Dearest Ruth!

Always a [illegible]!

The Song of Rahu

Love your whole life!

love

Kishori x

BONUS FREE EBOOK DOWNLOAD

A Gift from Kishori Jeanette McKenzie

The Call

An introduction to Living Alchemy

Designer Software for

the Evolutionary Mind

Tell Me What You Really Want

Tell Me What You Really Are

Discover Your Inner Spark

at

www.magick-makeover.com/designer-software

The Song of Rahu

Dancing on the Razor's Edge

A Contemporary Fairy Tale

Rahu the shepherd

The benevolent disruptor

Key to a harmonious life

Love your whole story

KISHORI
JEANETTE MCKENZIE

First published in Great Britain in 2022

First Paperback Edition 2023
ISBN: 978-1-7393094-0-4
Published by Mahadevi Press

Disclaimer: The impact of the content of this book may be disturbing. It is not intended to be a substitute for the psychological advice of a licensed professional. The reader should seek support from a qualified professional if required. Knowing that we are all One, all expression here about seeming 'others' are perceptions through my personal filters at the time, and the filters have now dissolved.

FEEDBACK ON THE BOOK

"Your book is pure genius! It's a masterpiece"

"It is rich beyond words, and I imagine the reader to find endless treasure here. What a gift of love!"

"It's turning my life around"

"Profound and ethereal all at once"

“I’ll be coming back to this again and again. It’s my new Bible”

“Simply life-changing”

“Epic and deeply moving”

“Such an important message for our world right now”

“One of those once-in-a-lifetime books”

“It’s an absolute godsend in the apparent chaos on our planet. After reading it, I feel everything is just as it should be”

“Kishori Jeanette McKenzie’s words are so wonderful, comforting and uplifting”

ACKNOWLEDGEMENTS

Cover Design by Andrea Swiedler
Rahu Image by Jane Adams Art
Graphics support by Locian

Thanks to all those who have knowingly and unknowingly played with the profound application of *The Song of Rahu* and welcomed the Atithi, since there is no Other; to my inspirational son Krishna (Duncan) McKenzie who initiated and produced the recording, and to my devoted and multi-talented editor Vanessa Squire.

Mahadevi Press
Tavistock, Devon, UK
rahu@kishori.net
www.kishori.net/rahu

CONTENTS

THE WAVE BREAKS

Refining the detail. Self-Inquiry is a messy game. Allowing the ripening of the fruit, sifting out the withered grapes, a few maggots pressed into the juice, as we relentlessly tread the pulp to the last drops of individuated experience. Everything written here, everything we experience, could also be the opposite. Whatever you look at, there is only one consciousness. There is no Other. The wave breaks.

Jeanette's role in this shadow puppet theatre is to be an alchemist, with love and passion, a catalytic converter, as Lao Tzu called me in a conversation we had in my inner realm. Revise the feeling first, or you'll get the old default. Over the years I have experienced a softening somewhat from **doing** into Allowing. Elegance rather than effort! With the precision of a Zen archer, never accommodating. Direct downloads from the Absolute, pointing at the Ultimate.

"Highest of High and Lowest of Low. Nothing to do and nowhere to go." These are the words spoken to me by Hermes Trismegistus, the thrice-great Master Alchemist. During this lifetime I have been gifted with life-changing words from several Great Beings, some who have lived in the physical, some on the Inner. About forty years ago another Master Alchemist Giordano Bruno told me: *"Your destiny is*

to know the Real from the unreal."

It has taken a lifetime to fully feel the gifts in these words from the depths. My perception was not yet clear enough to hear. Mind not yet surrendered enough to know we make up it all up. Especially valuable are the discordant chaotic notes as they impel us to make the choices for our new world. My Being told me: *"I have given you so many clues on this treasure trail, and you did not hear."*

"I was a hidden treasure and I wished to be known, so I created a creation," says Hadith. Meanwhile, lowest of low, my Shadow Baby Jane was deeply suffering, *"Bound like Chinese feet, to no longer know that flowing feeding, soma nourishing current of life that I am"*, says my Shadow Baby poem. She's wild. She's also my ancestors, stretching for aeons. She attempted in so many ways to set herself free, and me.

I discovered much during this last year, preparing this book for publication, in reviewing the mountains of my writings saved on hard drives, memory sticks, piles of paper, diaries and notes. On the pieces selected I've mentioned any dates or places noted to give some perspective, but most pieces don't mention dates – they're timeless.

Among the writings I discovered what I love, and what makes my toes curl in embarrassed boredom. The words full of feeling, *"Con palabras que fuesen a un tiempo suspiros y risas, colores y notas"*, which translates as "With words that would be at the same time sighs and laughter, colours and music", from the Gustavo Adolfo Becquer poem which touches my Heart. The cries of I and the conclusions of We! And in some of my writings I found I was not fully embodied. The dimmer switch of feeling is turned down. The transmission is low.

I also have a life of husbands, lovers and loved ones, my amazing children, my homes, travel and friendships. Those are a richness for another story. I have shared here a few footsteps, still vibrating, or not, with the presence of the one who walked in them. Personifying the spirit of Rahu has made this a love story, like '*The Coming of the Dark Ones*' (Pada 64).

Finally, a few points for those walking this path of alchemy. Desire is precious. It is both personal, and impersonal. The desire with which you incarnate is absolutely to be fulfilled. It's simpler when you allow. Fulfilment is the other side of the coin. Impossible to have desire, without fulfilment. The word 'desire' is from the Latin '*de sidere*', 'from the stars', and it is part of your destiny to allow fulfilment.

Desire is an arrow emerging from Source. It is a loop, and necessarily has to return to Source in completion. Our life is a story, a pantomime. At the end of the pantomime all the characters stand hand-in-hand to take their bow together.

Self-Inquiry, the alchemical process, is the *Hieros Gamos,* the great love affair, discovering true identity. It is the most wonderful contribution we can make to the harmony in this world play. The highest possible contribution, it is either easy, or impossible. Easy when we allow, impossible when we make effort. Self-Inquiry is the process of withdrawal of projection, and rearranging of the contents of the conscious mind, knowing there is no Other.

As I complete the offering of *The Song of Rahu,* along with some related reflections from my writings over the years, I am drawn to remember the words of the *Popol Vuh*:

"There is no pleasure greater than coming to life again after having been torn to pieces".

To conclude, how to live in times of chaos, transition, and times of joy? Allow the carpet to roll up behind you as you walk, consuming it all. Acquire the knack of gazing with the eyes of the Heart, curious like a baby. Relish your whole story. Let go of **doing**, and witness it all. The Heart consumes it all. The Heart feeds on it all effortlessly, alchemising distortion, spontaneously revising and rewriting with imagination, shapeshifting the magickal world as desire returns inevitably to Source.

Kishori Jeanette McKenzie
December 2022, revised January 2023

FOREWORD
by Gary O'Toole, Vedic Astrologer

I first heard of *The Song of Rahu* when I listened to Kishori recite a prelude online. I was immediately transfixed. The words themselves were profoundly moving, and shocking, and, at the same time, soothing and centring. But I needed more!

Rahu's typical astrological expression of disturbance seemed to turn in on itself in an instant. I later read on her website that *The Song* asked us to look at what seemed 'unwanted', as if 'steering into the skid'. While I was aware of Rahu's ability to challenge, distort and contract the mind, I had learned to shift my perception over the years. I just hadn't heard anyone articulate it so clearly, so joyously.

I had studied Rahu as an astrologer for more than twenty years. Thanks to Kishori, I would come to know Rahu as the 'illuminating dark lord', having only ever heard of the shadow that is Rahu as dark. It was because of her child-like curiosity that I could peek into the possibilities that lay beyond my conditioned responses.

The Rahu cycle of astrology had been dominating my life for many years (Rahu's major cycle lasts 18 years). It was beginning to loosen its grip as I came towards the end of the cycle when I first met her. She seemed to appear on the banks of a particularly treacherous river with words that guided and calmed my soul. At times, I had to fight back tears of relief while conversing with her for the podcast we went on to record together. And while my hunger for knowledge remained, it began to manifest as a satiation I had not felt before.

In just a few weeks after contacting Kishori, we began to develop a series of conversations, using the houses of astrology as a 'map of consciousness'. I was later reminded by Kishori that the "the map is not the terrain". I know how good a map astrology is, but Kishori was giving me a full-bodied, Heart-filled experience of the terrain.

After having completed the series of talks about Rahu in each of the houses of astrology for the *Timeline Astrology* podcast, I now feel I have been initiated into a secret language – a language of the Heart. As Kishori always advises in our conversations, "Put your hand on your Heart". I have been practising this when facing whatever mishap, or when things seem to fall apart.

Together with Kishori's words, the simple practice of placing my hand on my Heart has been a refuge. I have practised it in various scenarios and at different times. It centres me every time. Not only that, but it also brings with it an intelligence my intellect could never match. It is the intelligence of the "HeartField", as Kishori puts it. It reminds us of the stillness in all the apparent chaos. Rahu reminds us that there is a place for chaos, too. It is like 'rocket fuel', to propel us to the next great state.

As I continue to explore *The Song,* I realise its magick is in hearing the words spoken by Kishori herself. I am so grateful to have been able to converse with her. The wonderful sounds that emanate from her at times when I am fragmented, torn apart, are so comforting that I know I am in the presence of a true Guru, although she would never even claim to teach. She calls herself a 'catalytic converter'. I can attest to how effective and helpful her approach is. It has been a personal revelation and retreat, a homecoming. As an astrologer, it has enriched my practice, too. I can now offer so much more to those who seem to be lost in the throes of a fragmented mind, of Rahu.

I no longer see Rahu as the enemy. And while it can still bring the contracted states I used to dread, I now realise the opportunity. I know that the 'I' that I am is in everything and everyone. I can withdraw my projection and awaken to the full spectrum 'I'. Yes, it can sometimes slap me awake when I have ventured too far off centre. But mostly, like *The Song,* it lovingly nudges me awake, calling me back to what is real. For that, for the words Kishori imparts with such eloquence and reassurance, I am forever grateful.

Gary O'Toole, Vedic Astrologer
www.timelineastrology.com
December 2021

Gary interviewed Kishori for his *Timeline Astrology* magazine about *The Song of Rahu*, following their series of podcasts. https://anchor.fm/timelineastrology
Here is the interview:

The Song of Rahu **Interview – Introduction**

Kishori, Keeper of the Karousel, is a luminous dreamer of dreams and weaver of webs, superfluid shapeshifter, catalytic converter, spinner of tales, lover of the leela of life who never grows old. Super-contemporary creator of designer software for the evolutionary mind.

Gary's Questions and Kishori's Answers

What is *The Song of Rahu*?

It is an epic poem I wrote over 30 years ago, a catalytic incantation, a parable of realisation that love is all there is. Life is simply an expression of the nature of reality, adoring its own existence. Nothing can separate consciousness from itself. The best way of engaging with *The Song of Rahu* is to feel it with the Heart, rather than attempt to understand it with the mind. True clarity comes only when mind is illumined by the Heart. There is only reality to experience, and reality is one.

How did it come into being?

It was spontaneously gifted to me as I listened to

a friend chanting the 108 names of Rahu. I had an epiphany as I listened. I was shaking and weeping, and he urged me to sit and write. For three days I honed the words of the poem, and knew them into form.

Why has it taken so long to publish?

It was originally published about 15 years ago on CD, but it was premature. I have been reluctant because mind not rooted in the Heart is so easily scandalised. It is a transmission of the carrier wave of sound. The principles of truth are so deep that mind in separation from the Heart cannot grasp them. Different parts of the mind engage in 'understanding' the written and spoken words. The words are not set; I often will spontaneously use a different word as I allow *The Song* to be sounded.

How would you encapsulate Rahu in just a few sentences?

Like all the gods, and everything else, in fact, Rahu is the personification of a frequency, a catalytic force, a state of emerging. Rahu is key to newness where infinite beauty and clarity come into form. Humans are for the most part currently set in a default of habitual contraction and judgment around anything which displeases them. Rahu is the chaos of the state of change, prompting us to pay attention, all disturbance is the herald of something new. An invitation to choose what you really want.

Humanity is a transitional being not yet born.

We are creation coming into form, encountering Rahu on the roller coaster. Just like the process of transition in birth, and the swirling chaos of a turning tide, he reveals the inevitable union of opposites. We must have inquiry and allowing to activate coherence. Rahu is paradox to mind, reminding us to give attention to presence in the experience of absence.

What does *The Song of Rahu* have to teach us now?

Rahu is not 'teaching'. He is Self revealing to Self, calling us to be ready, to be curious. He is a catalytic force of nature, pulling the rug on all illusion, allowing our innate knowing to emerge. The words of the Song are self-explanatory; mind rooted in the HeartField is illumined and knows. We remember who and what we really are. Efforting of any kind gets in the way. "Sit rather in the middle of the house, love and understand the mystery of my dark secret ways," says *The Song*.

When mind listens without being rooted in the Heart, it struggles to understand. Rahu dances on the razor's edge, leading beyond experience to reality. He is the heartbreaker and shapeshifter. Suspending all 'known' logic, this is a koan, a puzzle, an invitation to embrace sovereignty.

How can people learn more about *The Song of Rahu*?

For bookings for talks, exploration circles and media enquiries you're welcome to contact me by email on rahu@kishori.net

For more than ten years I've been running a *Song of Rahu* page on Facebook https://www.facebook.com/SongOfRahu

There is a page about Rahu on my Magick Makeover website, with a recital of some excerpts: https://www.magick-makeover.com/about-magick-makeover/rahu/

On Instagram: https://www.instagram.com/song_of_rahu/

We are running recitals, talks, events and further explorations into *The Song of Rahu*.

See **https://kishori.net/** for more details, and as a reader of this book you're invited to join our private **The Song of Rahu Book** Facebook group www.facebook.com/groups/thesongofrahubook

WELCOME

There is a place, a way, a state we once knew, before and beyond space-time, and still know, that moment in the rose garden, a magic home, a secret paradise, an echo, that somewhere over the rainbow where all dreams come true.

That state in the fairy tales, there's a place for us.

Under the branches of Kalpataru, the wish-fulfilling tree.

It is both easy to reach – at the bottom of your garden – and impossible to access from certain states of mind. You can let yourself fall into it like Alice down the rabbit hole, but you can never get there by effort, and you will never discover it when identifying with conscious mind alone.

This is a magical timeless place, under the hill of the Heart. Love it, and it will reveal its secrets.

When we allow the merging of the inner and the outer, the above and below, the two become one, that secret door to the treasure cave opens wide of its own accord. We slip between the cracks in the world as we know it. We celebrate the relationship between the conscious and unconscious mind through Self-Inquiry.

Hold my hand and I'll take you there, says the Heart.

One who merges the inner and outer is truly a genie, a genius. I understand a genius to be one who has discovered their guiding light, their protective spirit, and is potentially able to facilitate any chosen desire with loving precision and satisfaction.

My language of expression includes many particular words and terms, especially from Sanskrit, defined in the Glossary at the back of this book. If anything is not clear to you, please ask.

HIGHEST OF HIGH AND LOWEST OF LOW

This is *The Song of Rahu*. It is, above all, a never-ending story, elusive, and can be tricky to pin down in prose since it is constantly evolving. Every time I recite the epic poem it is different. It is the recognition, and celebration as love, of all that interrupts and interferes with the chosen direction of habitual one-sided human consciousness. While we are actually the ocean, waves rising and falling, a pattern of drifting clouds, the only constant is change. Like mind!

When we surrender to **allowing**, rather than mastering, Mind becomes discipled to the Heart. All is One Love. Unwavering alignment to the heartbeat of **now**. We are the One at the point of arising. At this frequency Consciousness is designing itself; we are pregnant with our unborn Self. We are the cutting-edge choosers of expression, listening to the song of the never-ending love story.

Circling of the central point, the grit in the oyster, can seem repetitious in prose, the same themes reappearing. It is the disturbance, the conflict, which draws attention relentlessly to welcome the *Atithi*, the Sanskrit for an uninvited guest. Giving that tender kiss to what has been rejected as Beast. "*The stone that was rejected becomes the cornerstone of the temple*".

The Song of Rahu could be the Song of each one of us who chooses to play with Alchemy, undoing the cat's cradle of our world. Rahu is the Beloved Opponent, the Atithi who appears whenever the conscious attitude deviates from *'Keyala'*, from allowing spontaneity from source. When love becomes universal, embracing the whole story, it becomes deeply personal. No separation in the moment - from anything! Keyala. The neutral state, in the HeartField, our source home, where no distortion exists. No judgement, no assumption, no resistance.

Rahu leads into intensifying the movement of love in form, so in love with the unfolding story as expression, that no separation exists.And the rocks flow and the earth moves, and all form is empty of time. Conflict emerges in the human mind until we see, as Rumi says: *"One look from you and I see you in everything, looking back at me, those eyes in which all things live and burn."*

To transcend the conflict, the struggle of embodiment, mind must move to the superfluid state, allowing movement from the unconscious to rise and be loved and burnt in the fire of the Heart. Completing the alchemical process, the Hieros Gamos, the ultimate love affair with self. All past experience and thought are consumed in the fire.

The Song of Rahu is not just about the necessity of embracing the shadow, it is also my personal story of drive to get clarity and freedom from any type of apparent programming of pain and suffering. It led me to investigate the emphasis on love as pain, and the stories of the suffering Christ and the Saints, and the influences of my early years. My desire is to restore balance and sanity, to take the shadow of attack to the Heart, and witness the dissolution of history and archaeology in the body, while they are being consumed in the Heart frequency.

This is my personal story of recovery, of direct practical application embracing Rahu, the seeming shadow. It is a tale of my determination to discover Truth from my inner knowing, the paths and impulses I followed, and which daily continue to be revealed to me. Reviewing my writings over the years, I see how I crawled out of that imprint to realise we are truly capable of becoming what we already are. And that whatever appears to be our experience, it is always through our own filters. Only love expressing, in everything, as everything, bringing my conscious mind to really see what I have realised in my life. And this is for all who choose to emerge from the matrix of restrictive programming.

Honouring Rahu and the power of the shadow has taken me on a phenomenal journey, to be free from early indoctrination, and its influence over me. A true love story. No blame on anyone, it is simply my story of liberation from an old culture. I have come to realise how I discovered that **everything** is love by direct cognisance, and the way true individuation unfolded for me. I have no desire to hide any more! I now want to share my story, and how I did not go mad as I was dancing on the razor's edge. Time to play!

Since childhood I have been following the *padas,* Sanskrit for 'footsteps', steps of the dance to the tune of *The Song of Rahu*. Staying true to the alchemy in the HeartField. From the early years with the crucified Christ. Not recognising the miracles that were occurring alongside my intense suffering, yet knowing that they were completely entangled. That somewhere in my pre-birth ignorance and blindness I had agreed to this. I had failed to register the magnificent words describing my true identity. The contraction and pressure were unbearable. Physically I lost my teeth, and my posture, and curled up within, a little wild animal. I heard Hermes Trismegistus say to me, *"Highest of high and lowest of low"*. Exploring these polarities, this union of opposites, I qualified in Polarity Therapy as Practitioner and Trainer, and play with Polarity principles to this day.

Initially I did not see what was right under my nose as I was exploring in the wilderness. Gradually I allowed it all to be digested. Listening to and embodying *The Song of Rahu* was a profound turning point, the beginning of freedom.

A poem I wrote in 1988. Jane is the name I gave to an aspect of the hidden me, a true Rahu encounter:

SHADOW BABY

Jane,
Angry, angular,
Demanding, defiant,
Awkward elbows provoking,
Prodding, poking,
From inside me.

Undefeated
Despairing raging,
Tooth and nail
She claws at me
Her gestation generations long.

Years, aeons of padding
Preventing wrapping
Imprisoning, suffocating
She, crazed in her straightjacket.

Layers of billowing flesh
Fashioned a padded cell
to keep close
my sad shadow baby,
my inheritance:
Her rage increasing

Gathering, snowballing
Down the centuries
Gnawing at my mother's poisoned poisoning
guts.
Self-sacrificing, joyless
Shredding, twisting, rending...

She, resigned to a meek mask
Fraying at the edges,
Grandma's hand-me down,
A placid bleeding shell concealing
An endless crazy unborn chain
Of dutiful righteousness,
Mother to daughter
Daughter to daughter

Mushrooming
with each successive generation.
Is it my turn to hit the jackpot?

In the womb dark
She swells crimson...

Sweating straining
Heaving, groaning
I birth at last this monster child

Kishori Jeanette McKenzie
The Stables, May 1988

A drawing of Kishori
by an artist I commissioned (whose name I have mislaid, and would love to rediscover!) while at The Stables, around the time I wrote
the *Shadow Baby* poem

DANCING WITH RAHU

"Where do I begin
To tell the story of how great a love can be?"

There is one cause! In everything! There is one Being.

We could call that One consciousness. Love. Infinite living intelligence.

This great Magnificence!

In the divine play of realizing, Infinite Intelligence appears as all this. There are no false gods. When we give power to the 'how' we create a false god.

It is the I and the attention and alignment to This Great Identity in the Now that expresses and celebrates our choice, which permits no space for distortion, allowing the apparently magickal shifts and miraculous wholeness.

Bovvered?

I sit cross-legged on the floor in my tiny meditation room at the end of the gallery, light streaming from the skylight above my head. I am exploring the gap, the broken tooth, the absence in my left lower jaw, with that familiar unnameable feeling, a sort of puzzled, unhappy, helpless now what? Life seemed to me to be full of these endless confronting moments of interference.

Now what?

What am I to do about this? What shall I do? What can I do?

Mind ticker-tapes, miserably.

Mahadevi appears. Teenaged legs crossed beneath a bright red impossibly-short mini skirt, perched on top of an old grey, rather battered, filing cabinet to my left. She sits absorbed in nonchalantly buffing her nails, apparently not paying any attention to me.

"Grow a new one." She shrugs.

"I don't know how," I respond, not feeling any benefit from her advice.

"You will," she says confidently, and carries on, completely absorbed in shining her nails. I continue to ponder my predicament, doubtful about her confident words, and her rather dismissive tone.

She shrugs again, indifferent to my concern.

"Bovvered?"

I gaze at her, bewildered. She looks like that little filing clerk from an old British TV sitcom. Bovvered is her answer to everything! I feel a distinct lack of progress.

I am obviously unaware that she is the great goddess Mahadevi in disguise. Straight out of my inner world. Keeper of my files. Unimpressed by my blank response to her brilliant suggestion, she elegantly slips down from the cabinet and disappears.

I get up and go about my day, my inner hair shirt

feeling vaguely irritating. I didn't get it.

She and me. Me and she. My crazy bi-polar identity, as defined in the words of Hermes Trismegistus in his greeting to me when I first met him on the steps of the homing beam:

"Highest of high and lowest of low.
Nothing to do and nowhere to go.
Earth and water and wind and flame.
I Am That which has no name!"

I stand up and walk out onto the landing outside my meditation room, sunlight streaming everywhere, through the rooflights, filaments of sparkling light, dusty candyfloss.

How many years and how many forms it took in this game of life to really hear and feel *The Song of Rahu* calling me to radical withdrawal of projection! To realise this simplicity. The game of literally **allowing.**

The Song of Rahu is the Herald of interference, and the resolution. The call to radical withdrawal of projection. A love story, costing not less than everything.

"Quick now, here, now, always -
A condition of complete simplicity
(Costing not less than everything)"
- TS Eliot

I lost a lot more teeth on the way…

So many voices, and yet only One!

The White Queen dreaming impossible things before breakfast.

And Kailash Wajpeyi the Yogi I met in India, puzzled, asking me, "Why don't you do something?"

My husband Roy after he left his body.

Only one thing to see, only one to know. Only One, hints and clues on my treasure trail. My womb wall, my camera obscura, my world mirror.

Only One, in every voice. What a joke.

A house divided cannot stand.

The Never-ending Love Story

This week I have been speaking about Identity to those who are interested in what I am transmitting in Keyala Yoga. The Yoga, the Union in Equilibrium, the Blueprint and the Love Affair with what I am. That original face of the Beloved that we all are.

We all start this adventure of life with the same advantage. We are a flow of energy which is totally biased, an innate bias towards enjoyment, expressing what we already are. All the same identity. The same magnificent candyfloss of Quantum Impulse to shine and be the living intelligence of the infinite sun. The original Spandau, the heartbeat, the pulsation. We are the throb of life!

"I was a hidden treasure and I wished to be known," says an ancient Sufi text.

We live as a quantum mind, dreaming ourselves into everything.

No 'doing', simply allowing revelation of what we are.

No healing or mending or fixing!

Continually seeing, feeling, choosing what we love.

We are life artists.

A continual flow of becoming the **more** of love.

It is not a 'doing' from what has been, from the known, but a continual spontaneous welling up of newness.

Waves of the ocean of endless outpouring and dissolving. All is consumed and defined by what is arising. New every breath.

Dancing on the razor's edge

Redreaming form from space.

Shapeshifting in every breath. New with every wave.

"Now is the time of the unexpected"

The unwanted, the unseen, the unrecognized.

The moment of *"The last shall be first and the first last"*!

The jewel in the dung heap.

The alchemy of chaos.

Loving the unlovable.

The power of the powerless.

In my end is my beginning.

Where do I begin to tell the story of a love as boundless as the sea? How does love become what it seems not to be, so that there should be nowhere, no dimension unexplored?

Radical shapeshifting into occupying absence.

In dying we are born to eternal life.

The love affair of Mirabai dancing naked in the streets.

How does the unlimited become what it is not?

I stretch to the edge of mind at the *"furthermost reaches of the infinite resonance"* to be able to write anything at all. A thread trickling through time. Experimenting with my exits and entrances into this storyworld. Inspired from the unknown. Robotic? Or conscious entrances? The Spandau pulsation. The throb, the first faintest sense of a quiver in the muddy soup of potential. The uroboric inertia.

A tremble, a whisper, a breath.

Yesterday my Vedic Astrologer friend Gary, who has written the Foreword to this book, told me about the Sanskrit word *badhaka* meaning 'block'. Block is a closed door. And closed doors are for opening! Stagnation is a state already moving to flow, and discord is the other face of harmony.

I begin these words of Kishori for this introduction over and over again, ever fresh, new and different, the previous versions no longer energised, left feeling lifeless and irrelevant. I sit this morning in my unknowing, and begin to write again. What can I say about the Nameless One? My lifelong assignment of giving form to the infinite shapeshifter?

Turning the ball inside out, an inner assignment which I began exploring aged seven. My bungee-jumping into matter. "*Back bending, craning my neck to see,*" before the next wave shattered. Always seeking, curious.

Bubbling up, plopping back into the quivering mud of potential. This is the beginning.

The Kraken wakes.

Conceiving the inconceivable, a self-generated wisp of smoke swirling before the spark of duality, division. The one becomes not one. Gives birth to what?

The dream of separation.

"*I am the key to eternal life,*" says Rahu.

"*I was a hidden treasure and I wished to be known*"... so I created a magickal world.

I am the chaos of the New.

I stand on the cliff top at Varkala. Gazing out to sea, watching the edge of the turning tide. An eagle swoops in from the horizon, heading straight towards me, and caresses my scalp with his talons. I stand there in wonder, and don't have even a moment to feel shocked. I continue to witness the tide turn.

It has been an adventure, wandering through the echoes of my inheritance. This is a story for my memoir, "*softly sifting through the debris of the years*".

Time to begin anew.

I became Hercules diverting the River of Heaven through the Augean Stables.

Alice in Wonderland in conversation with the White Queen.

Sitting with children singing nursery rhymes. Ding Dong Bell, gazing into the well in inner space, curious about what is coming next, waiting for the trailer of our next movie. This one we have to write ourselves, consciously. Not from the well of the past, and beyond reruns. Something never before conceived on earth. The whole of existence holds its breath in wonder. What could such a creature be like?

Bearing the unbearable

Love your whole story.

Never regret anything!

As it says in *The Great Way, "Make the smallest distinction, however, and heaven and earth are set infinitely apart"*.

Where do I begin, to tell the story of a love so great?

In any footstep we can find the Fire in the Heart!

"The stone that was rejected shall become the cornerstone of the temple."

This paradox is in the integration of the shadow, inclusion of the wounded, damaged, rejected, unloved, unlovable. Loving the unloved. Bearing the unbearable.

Of the disabled, unwanted, unlovable.

This is the restoration of the temple.

And the valleys are filled, the mountains laid low.

"I am come to bring the good news to the poor, to comfort the brokenhearted and make the lame to walk, the blind to see,

I am come to set fire to the world, light a blaze in the Heart. And behold it is already alight and blazing".

Luke 4:18

Shakti, shakti, shakti,
Lightning, power, fire!
Heart waves
The tsunami

24/7 Magick Show!

It is so hot. I walk down the marble steps to the dusty street, my body already damp with sweat under my maroon robe. Too hot to wear undergarments.

I walk up the little back street leading to the German Bakery for breakfast.

On the left, sitting on the side of the road, is the little armless and legless beggar. He sits there every day. A brilliant toothless smile, joy radiating. He is a miracle. Such devastation and such delight shining, laughing in the face of his almost total helplessness.

Today another character in this movie is a street magician, sitting in the dust just beyond the beggar, playing the 'find the coin' game with three cups.

He calls me, "Ma... Ma... you want see magic show?"

I laugh, opening my arms wide, eyes up to heaven.

"Twenty-four / seven magic show!" I call.

I catch sight of the handless beggar grasping his coin tin, as if clapping his non-existent hands together. He is radiant! Our eyes lock, feeling the joke…

Shiva Rahu in yet another disguise.

Always in the Now, as I sit with the incompleteness of this story of Kishori's love affair with Rahu and the 'house divided' I read a friend's account of the horror of her illness, and then see other stories more friends have written of their own physical challenges... I sit and dissolve them, along with pain in my own body. A body which has played consciously with surrender for so many years. In my mind I wonder if I am experiencing the whole world's pain, since we all are One.

The Treasure

At some stage, 'I-We-Consciousness, Source' made it all up. We exploded into this awesome Never-Ending Story, the frequencies of the harmonious completion of the adventure buried deep in the unconscious.

A faint, almost- forgotten remembrance calls us to wake from our dream, our continuous visceral recapitulation of every part of our epic adventure of self-discovery. We remember! We realise ourself, integrate, make Real, every part in our movie. Hero and villain, lover and beloved, parent and child, we each play all the parts in our movie, and recognise this.

Laughing, we take our bow at the end of our pantomime. In the resolution of every conflict, every split, every separation, we remember Heaven on Earth and begin to Live in freedom, radiating to all, this discovery of the "Treasure hard to attain".

I am this shapeshifting alchemical transformation, and I continue to witness the never-ending story, every shining cell radiantly awakening to eternal life!

This is the uncoding of that mysterious line in *The Song*: *"Rahu is a poisonous snake feeding at the breast of the mother. She nourishes and treasures him, her changeling child, the malformed, the experience of difference."*

Love your whole story, it's all Treasure.
Rahu IS the Beloved.

MY OCEAN MIND

My ocean mind is full this morning
of vast expanses of sun-filled space,
whirlpools of light and seaweed flowing
in the currents and eddies
of this unbounded sea.

Limbs lying in pools of salt water
at the edge of sands
glistening in the sunlight.

I am the ebb and flow of life,
each tiny impulse
a longing to sing and dance
in the radiance of life's vast openness.

Seahorses flying in white waves,
floating in luminous warmth
of deeper currents,
dark caves in mysterious depths,
allowing, free, flowing.

I am a field of electrical pulse,
vast, unfathomable,
body formed from interplay of immense
currents.
Impulse to move and sound, feel and cry
cruelly conditioned into control.

Baby eyes and limbs and hearts
bound like Chinese feet
to no longer know that flowing-feeding
soma-nourishing
current of life
that I am.
I will no longer be bound
no longer imprisoned.
For I am the freedom of life
Yearning for myself.
Without this freedom
to dance and play and sing,
I am dying.
I will not live in this world as this world
with these restrictions.
For I am not bound
and I will self-destruct
unless you… allow...

But I am free
as white clouds on a summer's day
flying in the breeze.
Free as wild waves
crashing gales at sea
and ice floes breaking in the spring thaw.

I am free as dolphins playing
and I will no longer allow
this binding of my being
by rigid ways of conditioned thinking.

I weep for the loss of
my experience of freedom,
my child self imprisoned.
I am the free current of life
and I am the light of life itself.
I am the Heart unbound,
I am life longing for myself.

No more!

I am dying in this fairyland,
this heaven that I am.

I am the wild dark of night on the mountain
Snow on the hills
streams in the valleys
waterfalls in dry places
pools in forest glades
shade in the desert.

I am the wind stirring in the fir trees
and the scent of jasmine on warm evenings

I am the land of abundance
I am the earth awake.
I am the white bird of freedom,
I am I am I am.

I am sunlight on water
freshness of the morning breeze

first pink lightening of dawn
silence in the forest.

I am the juice of sweet peaches
sun-ripened on the trees
and the roar of the volcano erupting,
flowing hot lava over the land,
lightning flickering in the sky at night.

I give, I take
I am all that is.
I am the currents,
the tiniest impulses that flow as your body,
I am the anguish in your Heart,
the madness in your mind.
I will awake, I will be free

Now, here, I will be known as I am.
I am your tears, your anger,
your rage, your blindness,
I am all there is.

I am the bliss you feel
and I will not be bound.
I am a raging torrent
and the softness of feathers
on a bird's breast
And I will always flow.
I flow, I fly, I live, I feel.

I will no longer be
a toytown world
of robotic thinking
and dead eyes.
I will experience my freedom now.
I am the ocean of bliss
I am fire
I am the raging wind of change
I am the rising tide

Kishori Jeanette McKenzie

THE ADVENTURE

Bringing this book to you has been an adventure spanning more than half a century, actually before time began. Pinning down this powerful expression of consciousness has proven elusive.

It is a multi-sensory experience, a dance on the razor's edge. Hearing *The Song of Rahu* recited is an activation. The written word can be simply one-dimensional, whereas exploring the as yet unknown, the shadow, is based on **feeling**, which is multi-dimensional. The link to hear me reciting *The Song of Rahu* and the explanatory tracks is at the back of this book.

The recording was made when I was staying at a guest house in Auroville, southern India on the occasion of my son Duncan's wedding there to a local Tamil beauty, now the mother of my two Anglo-Indian grandchildren. He has been known as Krishna since he was 19 when he moved to India. One evening he came to tell me that he had booked a studio in nearby Pondicherry, and that we were going the next morning to record *The Song of Rahu*. He has great love for my poetry, and especially appreciates this epic. He is also a brilliant musician, and I asked him to add music to accompany the poem. He initiated and produced the entire recording project. I then sat up all night writing the explanatory tracks, and also asked him to find a

Rahu Pujari to chant the 108 Names of Rahu in Sanskrit. Years before, around 1987, riding a wave of deep feeling, the words of my epic poem poured through me over three nights and days, after hearing a ceremonial recital of the 108 Names of Rahu in the original Sanskrit. The story of the event is included in the recording (link to the recording is at the back of this book).

A life-long explorer in consciousness, I am constantly refining how best to share my realisations in a coherent riverbed. We are now in truly extraordinary times of transition, participating in birthing a new world. It is time to share *The Song of Rahu* and my love affair with the shadow.

Looking back through my vast collection of writings over more than sixty years I see that I have been consistently exploring these truths, honing my communications to what ears could hear and understand. Simple truths. Since my late teens I have been writing poetry and articles about my realisations. Much is written in diary form, with no thought of publication. There is no other – we are all one consciousness, and exquisitely, infinitely differentiated. Facilitating workshops worldwide for Heart Communication based on my experience as an Enlightenment Master; developing my Keyala Yoga as authentic movement and the embodiment of the four Yogic Flowers: Dharma - Purpose, Artha – Abundance, Kama - Pleasure and Moksha - Freedom. Above all, being curious and embracing the contradictions of life as enhancements.

My website www.magick-makeover.com has some of the resources I have built up over the years from articles, courses and events, and, more recently, on social media. The audio version of *The Song of Rahu* was recorded in India and originally published in 2007 on CD backed by my son Krishna McKenzie's music, but it has never been published in written form since the alchemical shift is almost impossible to capture in writing. The recited resonance of the poetry is key. What seems to be a disturbance is actually a doorway to truth.

I am now presenting a selection of these writings relating to my experience of Rahu in *Padas,* the Sanskrit word for footsteps, non-linear glimpses of moments in time, encapsulating feelings, experiences and realisations. The Mala of 108 Padas, the traditional number of prayer beads, are nexus points, drops of intensity, condensed seeds of clarity and feeling.

Now the time has come…

RAHU, drawing by Jane Adams

The recording of Kishori Jeanette McKenzie reciting *The Song of Rahu* text here is available through this password-protected link.
The password is **Mahadevi:**
https://www.kishori.net/rahu-recital

The Song of Rahu - Track 1

THE MYTH OF RAHU

Once upon a time, when creation was young, before time as we know it had begun, the Devas, the ancient gods of India, so the story goes, were setting all in place for the play of life to begin. They chose to make themselves immortal and began to make Amrit, the nectar of immortality, for that purpose.

One of the asuras, not a god, but a demon, was very curious about all this activity. In order to be present at the creation of the nectar, he offered to help by stiffening his body so the gods could stir the Amrit with him as a giant spoon.

When the creation of the nectar was complete, all the gods stood in line to receive their immortalising spoonful. This asura, called Naga Vasuki, slipped into the line with all the gods. Now, Vasuki was an asura, whose destiny in this play was to evolve as humans do, but he decided to take matters into his own hands, and skip this bit of his destiny.

When Vishnu - let's say it was Vishnu giving out the nectar - when Vishnu raised the spoon to Vasuki's lips, Shiva, let's imagine it was Shiva standing there, Shiva, realising the trickery, called "Stop!", and quickly raising his sword, chopped off Vasuki's head. But it was too late. One drop of the immortalising liquid had already fallen into the asura's mouth.

Now immortality is not reversible. It is an unchanging state. So now there lay on the ground an immortal asura in two halves. An immortal with the destiny of evolving. An unchanging being subject to change.

What to do?

The Vedic devas, ever practical, accepted the fait accompli and gave the head a new tail and a new name, and called him Rahu.

To the tail end they gave also a new name, and called it Ketu, and a new head. Separation and the flow of time had begun.

Rahu and Ketu were elevated to join the Grahas, the planetary deities that figure in Vedic astrology.

They were now the Chaya Grahas or the shadow deities, the north and south nodes of the waxing and waning, ever-changing moon.

Rahu became the significator, the focus for expansion and chaos. Pandora's Box. There is a tradition of fear around him in India.

His partner Ketu became the significator for

completion and liberation. But that is another story.

Embracing Rahu, the new, the unknown, the evolving, chaotic, raw aspects of life without resistance or denial, is to give the kiss of Beauty to the Beast in the fairy tale. The rawness is transformed in an instant.

That moment of pure response, allowing the motive of love to express, opens the doorway to a myriad possibilities. Lifts the spell of the mind on everything. Mind falls into the resistance-less space of the Heart and surrenders to the spontaneous impulse of love, and the experience of our world is transformed.

The Song of Rahu – Track 2

PRELUDE TO THE SONG OF RAHU

Rahu the merciless says

No amount of
Avoiding conniving
Squirming and skiving
Delaying and hiding

Guiltily lying
Deviously denying
Fearfully hiding
Slipping and sliding
Sighing and crying

For what is seemingly gone...

Or choosing preferring
Planning and scheming
Wheedling and pleading
Wheeling and dealing

Contriving and striving
Hurrying scurrying

Anxiously waiting
Avoiding or hastening
What may be to come....

Will ever prevent
The terrible event
That awful fearful
Reality blasting
Merciful encounter
With Rahu... Now

Since Now is all there is

The Song of Rahu – Track 3

THE SONG OF RAHU

Rahu is the Beloved.
There is only the Beloved
And Rahu is the dark radiance,
The dissonance at the furthermost reaches of the Infinite Resonance.

Rahu is the Beloved,
Humbly surrendering himself
To be the chaos, the wild,
Shepherding Himself back to Himself

Since there is only the One...

Rahu is the divine darkness.

And the love of Rahu for his own divine self is incomparable
Rahu is the humble servant of his own being,
the most loving of guides, the carrier of light,
The container for the perfection of the Beloved.
The most perfect point of transformation.

Rahu is the fullness of the One,
Most fully present in his seeming absence.
Rahu is the point of return,

The presence in the void.
Rahu is the living one.
Rahu is love.

In the discordant sound
Is the most perfect harmony revealed.
And the experience of Rahu is a gift,
A great blessing - love.

And Rahu laughs at who would limit him and see him as other,
For he is the Dark Lord who fully knows his own true nature.

He is the daemon, the trickster,
The One in his most pure expression,
Encouraging the wild and free display of life
Authentic and true, integral and wise
He allows no pretence, no deceit.

He is not lukewarm, he devours the unwary
Rahu is the living one, the Beloved.

Ice and fire, he is the extreme one
who dances on the razor's edge

Rahu is lack of ease, dis-ease
Rahu is one who is intimate with fear
The seeming absence of light
He is that light, hiding from itself
Revealing itself to Itself

Guiding the self back to the Self

Rahu is Pain and contraction and the fog of confusion and misunderstanding

Rahu burns, Rahu is Tapas
The position of extremity
Utter surrender – love.

Rahu speaks

I am pestilence and disease, famine, rape
And the scavenging dogs of war
And still I am the Beloved

I am chaos and disaster, change and decay
And still I am simply the Beloved

I am the sores of the leper, carrion crow and rotting flesh
The worm in the eye
And still I am the Beloved

I am death and destruction, betrayal and despair
And still I am the Beloved
I am the hot wind in the desert that destroys all in its path
The foetid breath of the lecher, the rapist's lust.
I am violence and murder

Discord and disaster
And I am the divine Beloved

I purify through my tamas
I am the one to whom all must bow, head to the ground

And the purity of my love is beyond compare
For I am the Lord of Misrule
And the impeccable servant of the living one

I am the devourer of duality
I am the glory in the experience of absence
I am fullness and emptiness

I am the glory beyond all experience
I am the destroyer of illusion

Search the deepest recesses of hell,
In every crevice under every stone
In the maimed and the blind, in the guilty

I AM THERE, I AM THAT **I AM**

Always eternally, prior to all experience.
I grind and devour and spit out the lukewarm.

I am fire and brimstone, eternal damnation.
Merciless, no escape, relentless, implacable.

AND STILL I AM THE BELOVED, STILL I AM.

I am the purifier, I am purity
I AM without opposite, without other
I am tamas.

The Lord of All speaks

Rahu is my dark doorway, my secret passage.
Rahu is a fast path, a slippery slope, the path of my left hand
All paths lead to me, all paths are me
And the path of Rahu is a tightrope, a razor's edge

Lies and deceit, a pit of snakes, a valley of scorpions.
And Rahu is simply my most beloved self
To be acknowledged and adored.
And treasured in the silence of the Heart

Do not scurry to one pole my children
As if afraid of the dark
I have no opposite
Be still and consider who I am.

A boat tips over when all sit in the prow.
Sit rather in the middle of the house.
Understand and love the mystery of my dark secret ways.

I am the lowest of low, the alchemists' stone.
I am vengeance and wanton destruction

Whore, harlot, libertine, the father of lies
And STILL I AM that I am, HEAR AND UNDERSTAND

I am the curse of cancer and of AIDS
These are my tools of torture

I am helplessness and loss,
confusion and misunderstanding
And the experience of poverty and lack

I am the lord of the flies and the stench of the charnel house.
And always, always I am the most high, the most pure.
ALL IS PURE, IMPURITY IS NOT.

I am relentless, merciless, unbending, ruthless.
Bend or break I will be acknowledged
In every form and in no form.

I will be explored through my secret ways.
Rahu is the key to eternal life, the missing link.
the untouchable, the sacred sacrilege.

Rahu is the serpent beneath the sole of the foot of the woman
The mother.

Rahu, Rahu, Rahu, Blessed is he,

Most glorious servant of Kali, herald of Kaliyuga.
Worship of Rahu brings instant freedom.
Rahu is a poisonous snake feeding at the breast of the mother
She nourishes and treasures him
Her changeling child, the malformed,
The experience of difference.

Rahu is the lover beyond compare
Who dares all for the sake of truth

He leads by the path of desolation into the ecstasy of freedom
He is the key to the union of opposites,
Fusion and melt down, Alchemy of the Heart

He dissolves the walls of the past
He is the darkness of the self
The final convulsion in the bliss of dissolution

Only those who are truly awake can perfectly acknowledge Rahu

He is to be honoured with integrity
Or he will swallow you whole.

He is the crack in the manifest world.
The sign of contradiction, the antithesis, the enemy,
The beloved opponent, the most glorious of

glories.
The coat of many colours, the purity of impurities

In the midst of filth he remains undefiled.
He is the author of mists.
The mist maker, the mistaker.

His children are grey and many,
He increases my vastness says the eternal creator

For he is my rule breaker, the destroyer of rigidity and complacency,
The eraser of pattern, the herald of night.
The one who most fully reveals himself.

The shatterer, the shaker, the earth quaker, the heart breaker,
The holocaust, the avenging angel.

And still he is simply My Divine Beloved.

The Song of Rahu – Track 4

THE 108 NAMES OF RAHU

as chanted by the Rahu Pujari

Rahu Astottara Shatanamavali

Om rahave namah
Om soumhikeyaya namah
Om vidhuntudaya namah
Om surashatrave namah
Om tamase namah
Om phanine namah
Om gargyaynapa namah
Om surapye namah
Om nibajimutasamkashaya namah
Om caturbhujava namah
Om khangakhetakadharine namah
Om varadayakahastakaya namah
Om shulayudhaya namah
Om meghavarnaya namah
Om krishnadhvajapatakavate namah
Om dakshinashamukharathaya namah
Om tikshnadamshtakarallakaya namah
Om shupokarasansthaya namah
Om gomedhabharanapriyaya namah
Om mashapriyaya namah
Om kashyaparshinandanaya namah
Om bhujageshvaraya namah
Om ulkapatayitre namah
Om shuline namah

Om nidhipaya namah
Om krishnasarparaje namah
Om vishajvalavrita asyaya addhashariraya namah
Om shatravapradaya namah
Om ravindubhikaraya namah
Om chayasvarupine namah
Om kathinangakaya namah
Om dvishacchatracchedakaya namah
Om karallasyaya namah
Om bhayamkaraya namah
Om krurakarmane namah
Om tamorupaya namah
Om shyamatmane namah
Om nilalohitaya namah
Om kiritine namah
Om nilavasanaya namah
Om sanisamntavartmagaya namah
Om candalavarnaya namah
Om ashvyriksabhavaya namah
Om meshabhavaya namah
Om shanivatphaladaya namah
Om shuraya namah
Om apasavyagataye namah
Om uparagakagaya namah
Om somasuryacchavivimardakaya namah
Om nilapushpaviharaya namah
Om grahashreshthaya namah
Om ashtamagrahaya namah
Om kabamdhamatradehaya namah
Om yatudhanakulodbhavaya namah
Om govindavarapatraya namah

Om devajatipravishtakaya namah
Om kruraya namah
Om gharaya namah
Om shanirmitraya namah
Om shukramitraya namah
Om agocaraya namah
Om mani gangasnanadatrenamah
Om svagrihepravaladhyadaya namah
Om sadgriheanyabaladhritenamah
Om caturthe matrinashakaya namah
Om candrayukte candalajati sihmajanmane rajyadatre namah
Om mahakayaya namah
Om janmakartrenamah
Om vidhuripavenamah
Om madakajnanadaya namah
Om janmakanyarajyadatrenamah
Om janmahanidaya namah
Om navame pitrihantrenamah
Om pancameshokadayakaya namah
Om dhyunekalatrahantrenamah
Om saptame kalahapradaya namah
Om shashthevittadatrenamah
Om caturthevairadayaka namah
Om navamepapadatrenamah
Om dashame shokadayakaya namah
Om adau yashah pradatrenamah
Om ante vairapradayakaya namah
Om kalatmanenamah
Om gocaracaraya namah
Om ghanekakutpradaya namah

Om pancameghishanashringadaya namah
Om svarbhanavenamah
Om balinenamah
Om mahasaukhyapradayinenamah
Om chandravairine namah
Om shashvataya namah
Om surashatravenamah
Om papagrahaya namah
Om shambhavaya namah
Om pujyakaya namah
Om patirapuranaya namah
Om paithinasakulodbhavaya bhaktarakshaya namah
Om rahumurtayenamah
Om sarvabhishtaphalapradaya namah
Om dirghaya namah
Om krishnaya namah
Om atanavenamah
Om vishnunetrarayenamah
Om devaya namah
Om danavaya namah

The Song of Rahu – Track 5

HOW I WROTE THE SONG

Here is the story how the words of *The Song* came to be written.

Some years ago, a friend who is a Vedic astrologer was living in my house. He was in the habit of regularly offering *puja,* rituals to the Grahas, the planetary deities, chanting their names and offering flowers and incense.

Sometimes I would be present for at least part of these *pujas,* although I was not a participant. I would just attend sometimes, if I felt the impulse.

On this particular occasion I went into the room and sat down calmly to observe, as I usually did. Very quickly, my body began to shake, and I started to weep unconsolably. At the end of the *puja* Andrew, my friend, was inspired to suggest that I should go to my room and write.

At some point, I don't remember when, I asked what was he chanting? The 108 Names of Rahu, he replied. It is his day. I wept and wrote, and communed with the energy which had visited me, off and on, for 3 days.

From time to time I would read some of what I had written, to Andrew. He told me that somehow the words and images that I had spontaneously received had been transmitted directly from the Sanskrit, and the images were present in the 108 names. At that time my knowledge of Sankrit was almost non-existent, and my knowledge of Vedic astrology even less. I had heard of Rahu, but had no understanding of who and what he was. To this day I have still not read a translation of the 108 names, and I am not sure that one even exists. So obviously I cannot confirm the accuracy of his statement.

The Song, however, does appear to have a powerful stabilising effect on those who listen with curiosity, and an open mind and heart. One of the many gifts that Rahu is said to give to those who give him attention is the removal of fear and confusion.

EMBRACING THE SHADOW

"*The Great Way is not difficult for those who have no preferences. Make the smallest distinction, however, and heaven and earth are set for ever apart.*"

So speaks an ancient Zen text (by Seng-ts'an).

Truth, like beauty, or darkness, is always in the eye of the beholder. To see and be simply that truth, whatever it may look like, is a choice to be made.

How we engage with the Shadow, the energy of the ungrown, the unevolved, the fearful, the denied, the violent, is the key to all so-called problems, individual or collective.

The habitual, unexamined reflex of fight or flight, attack or defence, thinking or strategically planning, does not work.

Conscious attention from the Heart simply gazes from the emptiness, like the eyes of a baby, and gives the kiss of Beauty to the Beast.

A little, almost imperceptible, shift in perception into the silent Now in the Heart, can transform everything in the moment, melting walls and miraculously changing outcomes.

When the eye sees beyond the surface and the outer personality, there is a concentration like a laser beam, a burning of the fossil fuel of our old programming, and the walls of the past dissolve.

When vision, however, stops at the surface only the reflection of old structure is experienced, and the full spectrum reality of what all this play really is remains unappreciated.

There is no other.

It is not difficult to see in this way. It is our natural state.

To see with the eyes of a child.

It takes only a little willingness and a little courage.

The Song of Rahu is a celebration and an honouring of the choice for radical withdrawal of projection onto the seeming, external world. It is a choice to see only the Beloved, with the eye of the Beloved, whose root rests in that silent neutral space we call the Heart.

And as we see it, so shall it be.

Bend or break, as says *The Song*.

This is the destiny to which we must all come, in the moment.

Melt or shatter. It is a choice for each Heart to make.

And our choice affects the whole of existence.

Breath by breath, embracing or resisting, we are all players in the Theatre of the Heart. Nothing, absolutely nothing, is personal.

Nothing is owned, not even our apparent, personal faults.

How are we to honour those who allow the shadow to be visible?

To come into the light to grow?

Only when it is conscious can it be digested. Maybe those who have the courage to cast a long shadow are indeed blest, as it says in *The Song*.

The Song of Rahu is a paradox. It is offered here with love and acceptance for all its apparent flaws and errors, by the Self, to the Self, from where it came.

"*Dwadiumastu govinda, diupiameva samarpaye, bhakti agranadevesha, prasida parameshvara*."

"Your thing, Oh Lord, we give back to you.
Your words, spoken by You, only to You."

Can we see the curiosity of Vasuki stealing the promise of immortality to become both god and evolving demon, as a hope, a calling to live consciously?

In the same way as we see Prometheus stealing the fire for man?

THE END

of the recorded *Song of Rahu* text which, as a special bonus for readers of this book, can be heard recited by Kishori Jeanette McKenzie through this password-protected link. The password is Mahadevi: https://www.kishori.net/rahu-recital

A MALA OF PADAS

Now follows a selection of 108 Padas, a Mala, a traditional string of prayer beads, footsteps in consciousness, non-linear experiences, nexus points, glimpses of insights and realisations I have collected over the decades exploring shadow. Each is *"one quintessential drop of liquid life, soma-flowing in the heart"*.

Some of the language may appear to be 'teaching' – it is actually me teaching me, Self-Inquiry.

This defines the Padas: Non-Linear Dynamic Living Flow rather than Congealed Structure. A form which is truly alive has a dynamic flow. It is a pattern of living energy, with rhythms and tides, ebb and flood like the ocean. The ribbed patterns on the sand merely show where the movement of the ocean has been. Consider someone walking on the beach. Feet moving one in front of the other. The footprints are already dead. They simply show where feet have been, like a carpet rolling up behind you as you walk through life.

Some of the Padas may seem like a repetition of the same point, perhaps in different words, from a different angle, emphasising – such is the nature of realisation as we explore. Until we get the punchline of the joke.

PADA 1
REALITY

Reality is… Already whole, radiant, pre-existing, only the **real** exists.

What creates the delusion that Reality does not seem to know and taste Itself in every breath is the veil of the conditioned mind, like clouds which hide the sun and give shape to the rays of light which penetrate our atmosphere.

It is intelligent, therefore, to observe and enquire about this substance we call mind, which shapes and conditions every experience.

The conscious mind is a tiny fraction of mind which is also the subconscious and unconscious mind, including what can be called the superconscious.

There are vast patterns of autonomous archetypal forces which, if we do not recognise and allow into consciousness, can control and rule our lives.

We have all already explored to some degree the Shadow and the necessity for observing and allowing this energy to evolve and be part of our life. We can look at the Trickster, this divine energy sometimes called a god, and variously known as Hermes, Mercury, Coyote, Loki which is so closely intertwined with the shadow.

The Trickster's assignment is to undermine the conscious attitude and trip and trick us into surrender and balance. With understanding and willingness maybe we can begin to appreciate, love and welcome that divine being which takes us down paths of wholeness which we would not otherwise choose.

We shall begin by reading, rereading and listening to *The Song of Rahu* to orientate us for this exploration.

PADA 2
THE EXPERIENCE OF THE NOT SELF

I begin writing this in total, wretched despair after descending into hell and experiencing complete and utter distortion, and my helplessness to resist anything.

I am crucified and abandoned on the cross of matter. I am become all that is reviled. I saw my only salvation was to be also the witness in hell, to be the living eye that reports clearly what it sees and understands from this experience. These worlds are the Bardos, the half worlds as described in the Tibetan Book of the Dead. The lands of the neither dead nor fully alive.

The individual structure of the human being is made up of a multiplicity of personalities, an array of fragments of frozen half-lived selves, some more dead than alive. Defrosting these fragments in order to absorb and digest them in present time is anguish which is often preverbal. The blocked horror, the raw violence of incarnating, of becoming flesh, of innocence embodying, begins to reveal itself. It is thawing out, releasing energy which is painful but inevitable, as the experience of limitation and powerlessness becomes accessible to the senses of the mind. The unbearable illusion and anguish of

self, of becoming Other. Separate, fragmented, shattering into shards, like the fairytale Ice Queen's mirror. Of becoming the Not Self, the Not One.

Each one of us is a whole universe of people. Each seed, every fragment, seems to be in dire need of salvation, of love, of being seen, welcomed and tenderly accepted and reintegrated. What is not accepted will create a tremendous pressure from within the individual system.

Each fragment yearns to live, longs for a saviour, a guru, a prophet, a messiah, a deliverer from death, a listener, a mother, father, lover, nurturer.

And every breath potentially births a myriad new beings.

Monday night, 23 August 2003

PADA 3
BEHOLD

March 2001

Behold, I make all things new. Today I am complete in the emptiness. Life begins anew. I am the guardian, the servant, the lover of this living flame that I am.

I am the living Ramayana. This is my story. This is my play.

My Sita was stolen by Ravenna who I now know to be Rahu, the Beloved. I experienced myself as the living fragility and fire of Sita in the strength of Hanuman's arms.

I know the safety and power of that holding presence.

Two days later in the Cascades car park, Portsmouth

Formlessness has arisen and taken form.
My Lord has compassion on his beloved.
Drawn by Parvati's tapas. Shiva wakes from his sleep.

I am the beloved of my Beloved. I am married to the Absolute.

He weaves the coloured rays, the gift of jewels from the nine planets, into a ring for my finger.

The wedding veil is stardust and my gown the sweet breath from his mouth. My flesh shines with his light. He anoints my breasts with the fragrance of sweet oils, rose, jasmine and sandal.

He blesses my yoni with his kisses and the full moon is a mirror for my face. The Earth, my daughter, he sets at my feet and he places a living flame in my Heart. For guests, all are invited and they are showered with the golden light of love.

The wedding feast is Amrit, the nectar of the gods, and I dissolve in the arms of my Beloved.

Thursday 22 March, on the plane to Kuwait

My head is forevermore at his feet. This is total bliss, to be at his feet where I have been since before the beginning of time.

This is my place - to be as the dust at his feet, the dust for which he has the same love as for all. I have come at last to rest, and am delighted to be as nothing. To let all be as it is and to rest in the unchanging, to rest in the Real. To allow the world of form to move and change as it will, according to the spontaneous play of maya. To see Him shining through everything.

I am full of wonder at the events of the last days. Truly Lord Shiva has arisen from his sleep and taken form for pleasure and joy.

The feet of Lord Shiva are exquisite, adorable. One touch of his toe is a treasure forever. 1 asked, some days ago, what is true devotion? Now I taste this devotion. I am kissing his feet forever. Just to see his feet and to lie there is enough for a lifetime. I cannot see this body anywhere else, but with lips to the ground at his feet.

He is pouring into everything. He pours his precious life, which is inexhaustible, into this form and into all form, through all the universes. He is in ecstasy as he pours himself into form, his beloved.

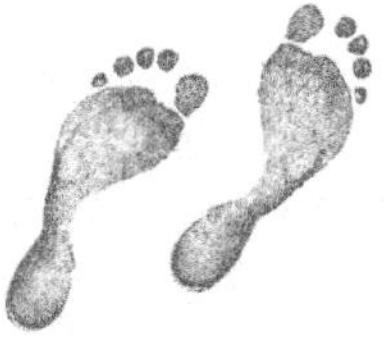

PADA 4
TREE LOVE!

All along the side of the garden there are some beautiful mature trees. A few days ago, I received some documents from the council. They want to cut the trees down. The thought causes me extreme distress.

I give attention to the trees and the possibility this morning, and I find the drama of cutting down the trees is embodied. In my body. There seems to be a deep wound in the dream of my structure which is resonating with all of this. I recognise it from other occasions of pruning and cutting down trees. It feels like the wounding of nature. The wounding of my own nature. My earth. I don't want them to do this. I feel it will be okay though. They will not get permission to remove them. I read all the documents online and I wrote a long letter about it to the council.

I feel that they will not succeed. There are conservation orders on many of the trees anyway. I am grounded in my choice. I looked at it all and didn't panic. I just felt into what to say. Best of all, I clearly saw the wound about trees and cutting and my own body. I spent a long time observing the situation with feeling attention in the Heart.

Russell phoned me. He is having some trouble at the Centre. I had wanted to look at the recent energy shifts in consciousness with him, and had emailed him to call me. I told him what I am currently seeing and experiencing. When we look at structure in the body and find and embrace the distortion, discover where it is embodied, we can take responsibility for 'external' circumstances, and can change or bypass them as unnecessary outpicturings of embodied states.

I saw that I can triangulate Heart and perineal floor. Then Russell said include the small intestine in this case. And Russell has to connect Heart and perineal floor and then liver for his own body. For these circumstances now of his swollen foot and the Centre.

Liver can regenerate itself. What is the significance of the small intestine?

Russell often tells me I told him all this before! Maybe so. But it is all new always! Another perspective, another discovery.

It's all in the body.

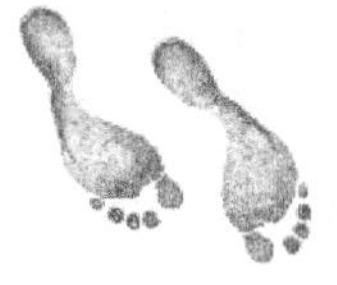

PADA 5
OCEAN OF BLISS

You are the Ocean of Bliss.
Body is a wave where you taste the flow of your bliss.
Baby is an unrestricted undulation of this Ocean.
Baby, the Beloved, the Lover, is what you are.
Allowing the wave to simply be the Ocean is Freedom,
Learn to live surfing this ocean.
Discover the source of your bliss and allow only THIS to open and fill the space you call YOU…
You are a garden of flowers.
Your life, the living fragrance rising from these flowers.
Enjoy the uniqueness of your seed and allow it to grow freely.
Discover the root of the Heart and patiently water this.
Everything is the Heart, a seamless womb delicately moulded to you.
Shape yourself to match THIS in every moment of life.
Become discipled only to the Heart…

Love is truly embodied, moment-by-moment, drop by delicious drop, as delight in what IS, right NOW.
As Nature, breath, nourishment, taste, light, movement, sound.
Gentleness, word, touch, sensation, flow, pleasure.
Awesomely consuming, and deliciously being devoured.
Surrendering to being digested, is truly orgasmic.
And what of your strategy, your rage, your grief, your loss, your fear, your pain?
Your discomfort, embarrassment, restriction, resistance?
Your perception of what is allowable, of what is possible?
Your judgement upon what you seem to be?
Your weakness, your exquisite vulnerability?
ALL is a great treasure, fossil fuel for the flame of life…
Everything is enormous potential for releasing energy to nourish the root of your bliss…
Learn the art of drinking the nectar which is distilled from the shadow.
Relish and celebrate every frame of your movie…
Awaken to the spaciousness which you are.

PADA 6
TEMPORARY GLITTER OF CONSCIOUS MIND

When only the viewpoint of the intellect is considered, when this conscious thinking mind which has been reflected to us all our life, creating the conscious personality we mistake ourselves for, we miss a vast amount of energy.

We miss the unchanging aspect of Being and are entertained by the sparkle of a tiny temporary particle. These little sparks flash in and out of existence like twinkling stars with the momentary existence described in particle physics. But without the underpinning wave of the Ocean of Life Itself we could not see the splash of the wave in the sunlight.

Mind polarises, focused and entrained by this tiny spark of conscious mind which is actually as helpless and unreal as a disconnected computer. It cannot function without the fire at the root of being.

The conscious spark is as evanescent and as temporary as a flickering particle without the sustaining wave of existence.

PADA 7
THE SO-CALLED SABOTEUR

When our conscious choices appear to fail, we (as conscious mind in separation) call this energy which works against the conscious intention, the saboteur.

As we contemplate the so-called saboteur we often fail to realise that our Being moves towards wholeness, not destruction.

It moves towards including all those aspects of our wholeness which, for one reason or another, have been abandoned like oxbow lakes, separating energetically from our river of life along the way.

PADA 8
CATCHING ATTENTION OF CONSCIOUS MIND

We, as conscious mind, see the experience of the undermining of our one-sided conscious direction as negative energy.

We take our stand against it, and the temporary sparkling mind fears it as an antagonist, when it is in fact the most loving of energies which can do no other than expand towards the full flowering of the whole tree of life.

'Particle mind' creates a divided house, at war with itself. We often feel we are going in circles or running a three-legged race in two directions at once. The dark side of our moon is that other greater, vaster, unknown depth of what we are. 'Particle mind' knows little of this, and wants even less to have such an inconvenient disturbing partner which is anathema to its illusory autonomous existence! This uncomfortable 'sabotaging', wonderful, dark, undermining, shadow side of life does everything she can to catch our attention in order to be involved in what 'particle mind' thinks of as its own possession. It is relentlessly emerging, like grass growing, evolving into life to **live** its own creation!

PADA 9
INEVITABLE POWER OF THE SHADOW

Unseen, unacknowledged, unaccepted, unlived energy is the very life force itself.

It is our vibrant, powerful, evolving nature, our sexual energy, our kundalini Shakti, our living life force itself. This nuclear force which is embodied at about one percent voltage, when repressed creates accidents, mistakes, pains and aches, illnesses, depressions and other 'undesirable' emotions, loss of interest and bodily disturbances.

How is this tension to be resolved? By simply embracing it all and watching it become one, whole. 'Particle mind' and wave both merged in the Yab-yum of the dance of existence.

Currently Rahu Devi lives out her disallowed power as abuse, terrorism, war and chaos. Like an enraged chained tigress, Rahu Devi prowls her world causing havoc, chaos and disaster. She is a capped oil well bursting out and spilling all around. If she is not appreciated for what she is, welcomed and allowed to live openly, she remains unevolved, unrefined, a chthonic projected harpy/devil, an energy to be feared or appeased by 'particle mind', which actually shivers in terror, knowing its collapsing house is built on shifting sand.

She is Rahu Devi, a Caliban, a living Tsunami, who must express her energy somewhere, somehow, and she does this creeping in the shadow, in secret, wherever she can find a crack in the conscious control to force her way through. A bemused, pizza-stuffing re-toxer! She is as unstoppable as a blade of grass pushing through concrete, a volcano which is ripe for eruption, or a woman in childbirth.

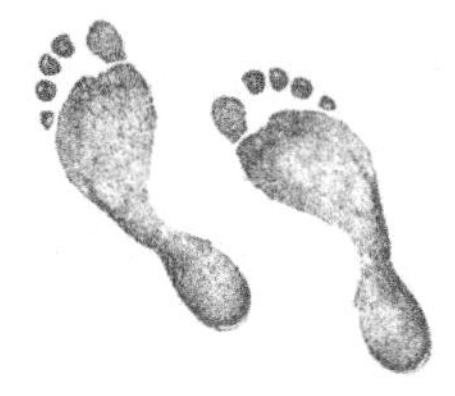

PADA 10
NUCLEAR FUSION

If this little conscious mind seed had the tiniest glimpse of awareness of the richness, power and genius available in the 'unknown', which is only unknown to 'particle mind', we would never move without consulting the Living Intelligence that is what we truly **are**.

Total humility is required, and this requirement becomes a demand when it is resisted. The mercurial arrogance of the conscious mind has to lay down its head in the Heart and accept that it knows only by the light of the Self, and is nothing alone.

Buddhi, intellect, is simply the temporary 'light at the doorway' which fades in the dawn of the Sun of the Self. For truly sustainable undivided **Life**, 'particle mind' must humbly acknowledge the true owner of this evolving Shakti-child of bodymind, and allow that nuclear fusion, that marriage in Oneness that is the destiny of Life.

PADA 11
SURRENDER

In the west the conscious mind has not stood much of a chance! The invisible existence, the vast pulsating reality beneath the thin surface film is not lovingly reflected to it, and so the mind believes it is lord of all.

However, the mind is also the beloved child of the Heart, and requires a language to interpret and translate for it. To show it how it is to be with the flow of life. So that the mind can see that this is **all** there is, a flowing wave, a rhythm, an endless pulsating bliss, not simply a glittering particle, a flash of sunlight lighting up the very temporary shape of the wave.

If the mind surrenders the idea of the cup and shifts identity to being the water within, changing and unchanging merge into One. If we can expand the experience of body, embodiment, fearlessly inviting in the unknown, we become everything. If we can be primarily the wave of life expressing as body, then the story of this limited ownership of life by the conscious mind is finished.

No more I, me, mine, or even ours and yours, an ownership which is all illusory anyway, a particle with no fixed or permanent existence. This is the axis which is shifting as evolution relentlessly takes place.

As Kabir says, cut the ropes of mind while life fills this body because this event can never happen when life is gone from the form.

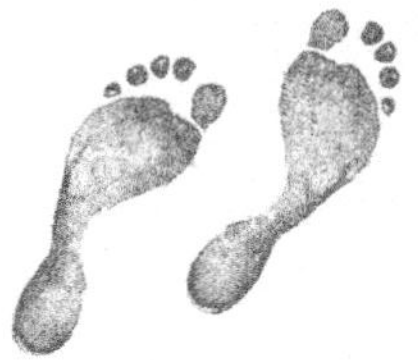

PADA 12
A CHILD AT PLAY

This is how we can understand what Jesus said about Mary having chosen the better part in the gospel story in Christian tradition of Martha and Mary, the sisters of Lazarus, who was raised from the dead. Mary sat silently in contemplation at Jesus' feet while Martha was *"busy with many things"*, cooking and cleaning. This is why Krishna distracted the Gopis from their husbands and their lives, and why Gautama the Buddha willingly sat for an eternity under the Bodhi tree. And why all distraction has been removed from Jeanette's life, for her to be hours and days and weeks and months in silence alone in this house, *"softly sifting through the debris of the years"*, says my poem. Life is contemplating Itself as it births its next phase.

This is what those considered enlightened have realised. Total simplicity. Oneness and death of one-sided identification with form. When the world turns inside out, it is irreversible. Mind bursts its tiny bubble for ever. The tsunami dissolves the experience of separateness. It can be seen that there is no longer an individual, whatever it may look like to observing mind. This superfluid flowingness - this is all there is. In reality nothing happens, and no one realises anything. There is no individual to realise. There is no Other. Life is doing it all itself.

Any final traces of the idea of personal ownership of mind were in the process of being digested.

This world is all my own form, and I am the Infinite Dreamer who dreams a beautiful fairy tale, with all the characters in my pantomime hand-in-hand in the world of happy ever after.

The Parousia. Paradise Garden.
I am a child at play.

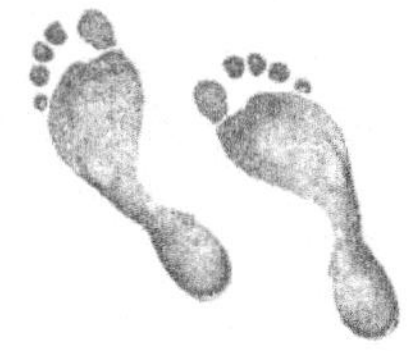

PADA 13
LEELA – PLAY OF THE ONE

I am
a hologram
A hollow gram!
A tiny lightweight, paperweight,
a zero,
a little empty cylinder,
which when you consider it
weighs nothing at all!
I am a hologram
a holographic, pseudopodic periscope
which the divine child
from her eyeless blissfulness
extends
in curious contemplation
of the latest configuration
of her bodily display.
An ecstatic probing finger
lovingly exploring
the thousand thousand faces
of her kaleidoscopic universal form.

What shall I be today?
In peals of delighted soundless laughter
The Radiant One

dissolves the passing Son et Lumière
this pantomime of light and sound
the fleeting magic show,
to rest in perfect silent Formlessness.

Kishori Jeanette McKenzie

PADA 14
ARE YOU READY?

Once we are willing to fully accept that everything we experience in this life, without exception, all those things we rebel against, criticise, despise, resist, hate and struggle with, we have ourself allowed, even invited in, then we are beginning to embrace the Shadow.

All the lovely things also that might seem to be in the lives of others to envy, these too. All the fighting against control, the wars and battles... the abuse from self, or seemingly from 'others', the neglect, the loss, I did it all.

This can be unbearable at first to open to, to own, not simply accepting that it is so intellectually, but deep down. Being this mess, this horror, interwoven, embodied. Feeling it, digesting it. I am the abused, and the perpetrator of my own destruction and my despair.

Realising and tasting this can feel like sitting in hell, with no escape ever. And I did this, allowed it. All. I made it all up. This play is mine.

But as the *Popul Vuh* says, '*There is no pleasure greater than coming back to life again after having been torn to pieces*'. Dedication to Self-Inquiry implies a recognition and acceptance of all projection, and a commitment to radical withdrawal of that projection.

Assuming our true identity as Operant Power and Source of our life brings freedom. And ability to emerge from this robotic self-created Matrix. And simply **imagine**. From the state of Yoga, union in the Heart, Coherence and Wonder. Beauty and Wholeness. Peace and Magnificence.

Shadow, that dark matter over which it might seem we have no control, this is our most Beloved Opponent, the key to our freedom. Practise Self-Inquiry, radical commitment to **see,** and discover, and know. Rahu surrenders to the Heart.

Do you feel it moving to embody?
This great mystery of the Shadow?

PADA 15
NOTHING OUT THERE

Your Life is One.

You are dreaming all there is.

It may not seem that way to mind in separation, but it is so.

Inquire and discover for yourself how this is so. Nothing is 'out there'. Quantum physics 'suspects' it to be so! What is Real?

In the HeartField, "*out beyond ideas of wrong and right doing*," says Rumi, conflict of any kind simply does not exist. There are no battles between good and evil, so no possibility of struggle or fight.

This realisation can be the release for all.

Realise and discover freedom. As you see this game, so shall it be.

See clearly, and what you see, is the way it is.

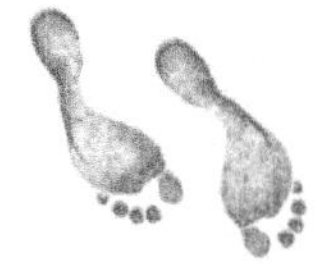

PADA 16
THE UNINVITED GUEST

Embracing the *atithi*, a Sanskrit word meaning the uninvited, unexpected guest, causes an immense change in energy.

Welcoming what has happened, as if we had chosen it consciously, causes a miraculous shift in what can happen. Resistance emphasises what we did not consciously choose in advance. Love what seems inevitable, and it transforms. What happened when Beauty spontaneously kissed the Beast in the fairy tale? It doesn't mean an attitude of tolerance or accommodating, but a genuine embrace of loving compassion.

Remember the inner action you can take whenever you perceive lack or distortion. Gaze steadily with the eyes of the Heart! This is transmutation of the perceived lack, and activates the flow of love. Place your hand on your Heart, and allow love to replace what you see, with the eyes of the Heart. You allow the real to shine instead. Gaze with compassion, see the experience, and allow it to shapeshift. With your intention, imagination and compassion of the Heart, you choose instead to see and feel and know the Real: coherence, beauty, abundance, order, fullness. All experienced absence, sorrow, grief, pain. and abuse are immediately gone. In its place you define joy, fulfilment, flow, wonder, love. You recognise Rahu for what he really is! You are the power of the Heart. There is no other. Know Shadow for what it truly is. Play with this until your eyes remember that they are the Power of the Heart, and can choose to see the Real.

The Beloved Opponent. Union of opposites. Matter and antimatter. Alchemy of the Heart. Embrace and include all expression of Shadow, and the conflict is transformed. A house divided cannot stand. A simple shift of perception changes everything. As Within so Without.

So, what is a virus? How did consciousness draw this distortion into form? Include all expression. Change perception. Embrace a Magick Makeover, and the conflict vanishes. Mind does not believe it, and so dismisses the obvious. Unite the opposites and Fear Is Not.

You want a solution? Ask for it. Let go, and relax into the state beyond the requirement for protection.

Rest in the attitude of true power.

PADA 17
AN INVITATION

What if unwanted disturbances, chaotic situations and catastrophic events, such as illness, accidents, violence and conflict are simply interventions and calls for attention from the unseen, moving to come into conscious awareness?

The Sanskrit word *'atithi'*, the uninvited guest, the unexpected visitor who we make welcome, describes these interventions well.

Much can be resolved by regular practice of Self-Inquiry, which reveals illumined mind, and body, and so authentic Life.

Invite the unnoticed, unseen, unacknowledged into conscious awareness, embrace shadow, withdraw projection into the Heart, where conflict simply does not exist.

"Until you make the unconscious conscious, it will direct your life, and you will call it fate." - C G Jung

How does that feel? Realising that we live as a house divided when we experience what we do not seem to desire?

I invite you to examine all shadow carefully. How am I inviting this *atithi,* this unexpected guest, to visit me? What gift does he bring?

PADA 18
LOVE AND THE LAW OF ONE

Be only love. Radiate only the presence of love in all. Notice when you use love as a weapon against itself, against your own self. Notice the distortion you are creating by twisting love and using it to hurt yourself. This is all there is to know.

When you notice a distortion, gently embrace it and release it. This is the open secret of living authentically. Live in love. Be the presence of love and shine on everything. Stay conscious. Pay attention to when you eat poison mixed with love. Poison, destruction originates as love, and is also only love, but as you twist anything, as you choose it to be, it will flow in the direction of sucking and leaching, rather than nourishing and enhancing.

The Heart never does this. It spontaneously brings all to balance.

Words are a case in point. Your individual template shapes how your hologram receives love. As disturbance, or as nourishment. To live authentically, taking responsibility for your life, to create the effect that you consciously intend, align your template to express only love. Root out the distortions. EFT, Emotional Freedom Technique, is a great tool for this. There are many other ways.

Simply noticing what the unconscious setting is, and dissolving it. Noticing the split in your structure, and making a conscious choice to energise only love. All the time. Twenty-four-seven. Every breath, every action, every thought, to bring loving expression to your creation. Take responsibility. If not, you are turning love into poison and using it against your own creation. It is unsafe to energise your distortion.

This is the radical answer to disturbances of metabolism and food intolerances. Eliminate systematically all that is appearing in your life as unlove.

Ho'oponopono, A Course In Miracles, systems that are based on love alone, on perception shift. On radical withdrawal of projection. All help to anchor love.

Quantum Heart is a simple way of sorting the wheat from the chaff.

The higher your frequency, the more disturbing the poison can become. And the swifter and more insistent the so-called karmic retribution. Like the tower in the tarot.

Nothing strategic will ultimately work to create your conscious intention. Control doesn't work.

Entropy always sets in. Boredom, distraction, forgetfulness, accidents.

This is how you can resolve all questions of nourishment. On all levels. Look at the programming, and systematically undo it. Don't use food as a weapon against yourself. Undo the programming before you eat.

A man cannot serve two masters! We often attempt to go in two directions at once.

Live expressing only love. Notice the results in your life, and see where you are allowing the old template to function. Live your Keyala, and all will be heaven.

Action has to be enough to demonstrate your desire, and not so much that it becomes a burden. Remember CS Lewis' tale of the fruit on Perelandra. And the words of Jesus, *"To him that hath, more shall be given, and from him that hath not, even that which he hath shall be taken away"*.

Whoever flows as the river of life will become abundant and fertile as the Ganges.

A river which does not flow becomes stagnant water.

If you move in the direction of the expression of love, all will unfold harmoniously. If there are unresolved hidden templates of twisted programmes, bugs in your system, then take note, and eliminate them.

Every breath, every thought, every disturbance shows you where to clean. It is like the Augean

Stables. Intend to divert the River of Heaven through your life, and you will definitely complete this Herculean labour of love.

Devotion helps. Love something, someone, some form opens the Heart.

Alchemy is a long painstaking labour of love, and you may begin over and over again, but the intention is to succeed!

Fill your house and body and cells with love. Without beginning, God is creating Heaven and Earth.

It is all without beginning. It is Now, and will always be, without end. Embrace with ecstasy the whole story, and poison immediately ceases to be experienced as poison.

Rahu is most certainly the way to go! You are being widened and widened to infinity.

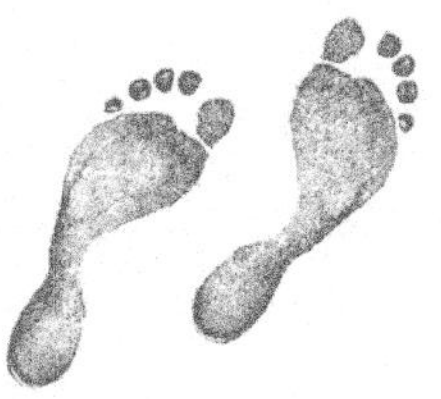

PADA 19
BEAUTY AND THE BEAST

Always playful, I call on the popular fairy tale *Beauty and the Beast* to explore the transforming power of the Heart. Beauty's Heart opens in compassion when she sees the dying Beast. As she kisses him, the Beast becomes the handsome prince, and the world reconfigures for them.both

This story is an invitation to a practical inquiry into living with vision and grace in these turbulent, transitional times.

For individual and collective evolution and happiness, it is vital that we allow into consciousness, and own, our shadow material. Continuing to project the shadow and choosing to identify with 'goodness', rather than wholeness, perpetuates the increasing polarisation, the alienation, terror and abuse in our world, which no one consciously wants.

How is this happening?

The Song of Rahu material arose spontaneously as a counterbalance to this error of perception. The shadow of rape, disease, obesity, starvation, lack of empathy, estrangement, terrorism, absence of authentic education for our children, control, torture, abuse of individuals and the earth and more. All these shadows lengthen with projection, and a lack of understanding of what everything actually is. Our world often appears possessed by a crazed, destructive archetype.

"*The psychological rule says that when an inner situation is not made conscious, it happens outside, as fate.*" - Carl Jung

So be aware! Pay attention! Investigate! What unconscious inner attitudes are giving rise to the situations we experience?

"*Man, if thou knowest what thou dost, thou art blessed, if not, accursed and a transgressor of the law.*" – as Carl Jung often quoted from the Bible.

What can we 'do' about it all? This is so often the question I am asked.

We can inquire. We can practise the simplicity of Heart Inquiry. We can discover what we are unconsciously transmitting, and in the process this transforms. We can allow the darkness, the unseen, into consciousness, to become visible. We can research what is happening in this tiny bit of the universe which we call ourself, that we appear to be in charge of. We can investigate our minds, body, feelings, and the events of our lives. We can explore with curiosity what may seem to be out of alignment: our relationships, our bodies, what we perceive to be falling apart in this world.

We can courageously invite the shadow into consciousness, and so release it from the inevitability of blind, robotic automaticity.

There is no higher service to our Self, and to the world, that we can offer.

We can practise Heart Inquiry.

The Heart is the Way. The human Heart filters and transforms automatically, enhancing what we love, digesting the fossil fuel of the shadow

Living from the Heart, embodying the Heart, communicating from the Heart, seeing from the Heart, moving from the Heart. Being the body of the Heart. Allowing the Heart to transform the unconsciousness which appears to threaten our world, and every one of us. This is true Alchemy of the Heart.

We don't need to strive to be complete, to be perfect! Even if it were possible! This is yet another delusion of the mind. We can simply choose to begin to consciously embody the Heart, and allow the transformation to unfold, becoming what we already are.

Opening the eyes and ears of the Heart to see what you are transmitting, to recognise the true nature of everything, is the way to transform your life, and that of the whole of existence.

PADA 20
REACHING FOR COMFORT

Why can't reaching for comfort work? I have been reflecting on how to speak about why I cannot reach out for comfort, but only in expression, for contact. My friend asked what about a child reaching out, and I know I didn't express it all to my own satisfaction. I want to speak of this from **experience**, not principle.

If I reach out from need or want, desire to **get** something, I am imagining I don't already possess it. And it is like attempting to reinforce a false belief in the reality of an illusory situation I am currently experiencing. I am attempting to confirm a false belief. I am reaching to **get**, to fill an illusory emptiness. As it is completely untrue, and what I am currently dissolving is false beliefs, I am going against the true expression of my nature which is simply to be the witness in these dark places in order to dissolve them in my being, not to reinforce them. If a child, or even Jeanette spontaneously as a child, reaches out without thought, that's ok. But when I am fully conscious, even in hell, and I knowingly reach out for comfort, I keep myself in prison. Disempower myself. Contact from where I am has to be for expression, not to fill a perceived painful emptiness. This emptiness is illusory, however real it feels, and can absolutely never be filled. There is nothing of substance out there. I can get nothing this way. First I must dissolve the emotional contraction, shift perception, and then I can make contact. By making contact with myself in the body I can make contact with my friend. I have to look back into my own source to find anyone, and as I look back into my source the contraction fades away.

It's not even a choice I can truly make any more. The energy is just like this. I may want to reach out, but if I am reaching to **get** then I have to somehow process this error myself first. If I reach out there to **get something**, it has no substance. It is like reaching for a dummy made of cotton wool. Remember, I said that trying to contact my friend from a place of demand was like reaching into cotton wool.

The object or experience I reach for falls away, becomes unreal, and there is absolutely no satisfaction. Like experimenting with reaching for my friend's hand yesterday. It is a bit like a demand, or believing in being a victim.

Now if I believed in the solid reality of everything then it wouldn't hurt to do this, and I **might** be able to do this and get some satisfaction. But to reach out for a dummy for comfort doesn't work any more when the consciousness sees it differently.

It is all a dream. This is not a personal thing. As consciousness I am moving to stabilise completely. It seems as if Jeanette is being trained to stay still and witness and digest anything.

I remember listening once many years ago, in my early twenties, to Fritjof Capra speaking at Caxton Hall in Victoria Road, London. Afterwards I stood outside looking at Westminster School opposite, and I knew at that moment that human beings are designed to be able to stand in the face of a nuclear explosion, and remain unmoved.

This is how I experience these principles. It is not a personal or a mental stance, it is a living experience. These are the bardos now! These worlds, now! Somehow I am being moved to match all my experience with what I know. To close this little gap between the accumulated experience, and what is true. It won't take too long!

Energy appears to go in two directions. In fact it can only flow in one, that is out into expression, and in this way return to source. It can only radiate. It is untrue to attempt to suck it in to a black hole which can never be filled. And this is what an organism does with a parasitic sucking emotional body. Attempts to feed illegitimately off others when its own source is there to nourish it absolutely. And it doesn't work because there is no substance out there.

I have this fantasy, it's as if I am merging an uncompromising, aware, disciplined Zen master with this little skinless baby! He doesn't seem to know too much about being vulnerable and is having to learn to be in apparent chaos, and learn the ways of communicating through tenderness and blindness, and the baby is a vast, sucking, empty rawness that doesn't even yet know the direction to look in for nourishment. She is like a drowning child gasping for air, and all she has to do is let go! He is attempting to show her how to truly feed, and he can only show the baby by becoming himself helpless long enough to find a common language in which to communicate!

I get the opportunity to experience and practise it all – blind!

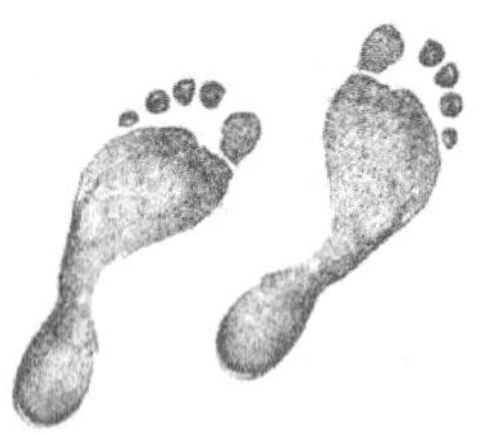

PADA 21
CHRYSALIS

A chrysalis. Humanity is transmuting. A pit of snakes lies writhing in the dark. An octopus struggling to free itself.

It does not have to struggle. The process is happening spontaneously, of its own accord. It thinks it is trapped and it is panic stricken, but the process is not under its control.

A gentleness is streaming from within. Change is happening relentlessly. Freedom is coming. I am freeing all from within.

All is Me, all is Me. One Being lies breathing, one Being sits watching. Humanity is one. I am setting My people free. One growth, one Being, One. Time to change.

This is My Being, setting Myself free. These tears, this allowing, is **my will**.

I will no longer be chained by rigid thoughts and prison bars, iron patterns of illusory beliefs. I will no longer allow myself to be prevented from **living**.

Time to change, My child, time to allow the freedom, time to come home to Me. All this is My Being freeing Itself. Freeing the world. Freeing you.

The birth pangs of a new creation. Behold I make all things new.

The ego does not exist. Soon the last illusory traces of this mechanism will disappear from the earth and allow Me to awaken the sleeping dragon, and transform My offspring into the Prince of Heaven.

The whole pot-boiling massa confusa will awaken into eternal life, the True Good. All, all consumed in the fire. All awakened. All to know Itself as Me.

All, all, all.

Just allow, **allow**. I do it all. You have nothing to do. There is only Me. Let it all go. Mankind is consciousness transmuting, awakening. A new life form. Behold I make all things new. A new creation.

I am not limited. I never have been. Egos, my poor deluded children, imagine they are responsible.

Ha! Egos don't even exist!

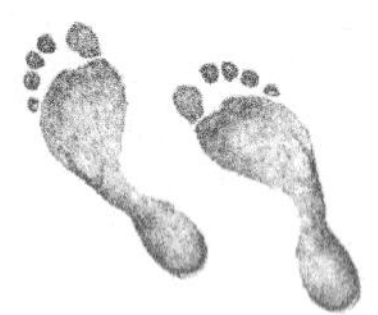

PADA 22
HIDING

I see that I have almost always been in hiding; this organism in some sense defending itself from attack. Crying "leave me in peace to breathe". From my childhood hiding in the long grass behind the house making nests to cover myself, and hiding in the back of the wardrobe, under the bed, behind the coats in the hall cupboard. Something just wants to be left in peace. I would hide my story book under the desk at school to be allowed just to read my story. I wanted fairyland.

I hid in The Stables, my beautiful retreat centre miles from anywhere, in India, in my parents' house, and now at the Quiet Mind Centre. Now of course my body is not so strong and fit, and the fat and pain prevent me from moving. I hide inside this body. I feel I never grew up. Something is relieved when those who make demands on me go away. I was partly relieved that, at the time, my children appeared to have abandoned me.

Yet there have been many successes. In spite of this attitude, I have made some original statement in this world… it could be enormous because of the clarity of my mind, and the willingness of my Heart. But unconsciously I built a wall around me, and let in those who saw me and my fairytale mind. I sensed I was not equipped for the hustle and bustle, the cut and thrust of this world. And so I allowed myself to be taken for a ride. I have felt like an old sow with her teats hanging out to be sucked! A leaking pot. My boundaries shot.

No wonder I wanted to hide. This must have been the cause of my exhaustion, and lack of energy to make new groups and ventures. My body did not appear to be responding quickly to my conscious efforts to bring myself to balance, to 'heal'. I sense I was still in shock from all the death and 'betrayal' – abandonment - over these last years, and I was exhausted.

Something in me wants a new way of life, to simply be a child, does not want to fight, loves to see the beauty and impulse to create in others, will do all it can to nurture these tiny shoots, often in silence, behind the scenes, always giving itself away in love, flowing towards this beauty of spontaneous desire, feeding it with attention.

I am integrating, all energetic projection returning to source, returning to that uroboric state of fully nourishing 'this one'. There is no Other. This I know. *Tat tvam asi.* Thou art that.

I want clarity about this 'neuro developmental delay'. What does that really mean? Why did this body develop with this massive sensitivity? Of what benefit is it to the whole? How does it serve to hold back? I remember Frank Natale asking me once in a seminar why I hold on to the energy, and looking at me and considering before saying, "Oh, I see, you are trying to heal. That's OK, as long as I understand".

And Manuel Schoch saying that I would not have to do what I told my clients to do.

I did not fully see why there is so much clarity, yet so bound by inherited structure of defence. In the archaeology of this body fear prevents, wraps, binds the essence. The stress of experiencing what seemed to be my mother's pushing, prodding, invasiveness froze and, paralysed some vital impulse. I was born into this, somatised it. Acquired the habit of stealing time for doing nothing, playing cards on the computer, just happy to stroll through life. It's not really fear as we might see it consciously, but a stubborn unwillingness, inability to rush, push, a reactive response to how I experienced my mother. I expressed an ingrained slowness, a defended dreaminess. I daydreamed through my childhood, building walls to keep out those who did not appreciate Jeanette. Hiding in shock, carving out a little safe place to live.

And now, at this stage of my life, how to change? I want to dance and shine! Like a child. Madonna would be a great image of my shadow! My body appears to sometimes be sluggish, pain strong, limbs tired and hurting. Yet I still know myself as Kishori, the silver-skinned martial artist, slim and super fit, a warrior goddess!

To bring anything approaching this into form I am aligning with this superfluid state. I call on the assistance of Proteus, the shapeshifter, original and mercurial old god of the sea. Wrestling with him is like wrestling with Jacob's angel. I demand that you appear in your rightful shape. **Now**!

I am creating this shift by magick, holding the focus, choosing a new state, another expression of this life. 'Doing' is very tiring, like attempting to clear the Augean Stables!

I imagine being a martial artist, dancer and singer of Life! Kishori Devi Khulchik!

My focus is extraordinarily precise, and everything is gathered into this laser beam of creation. I am giving birth to my opposite. I am shapeshifting. Now. Everything is subordinate to this.

So I create my support team. I begin to invite my meme of nine for today. Easy really. Madonna, Proteus, Hermes Trismegistus, Randolph Stone. I feel others lining up.

All dark forces are projection from the mind. Inertia and inaction are concentrated subtle frequencies. They seem to hold the life force prisoner. But I am already Arjuna on the field of battle.

I have to act, and I do nothing. Prisoner of the dream of inertia, and darkness.

20 August 2008

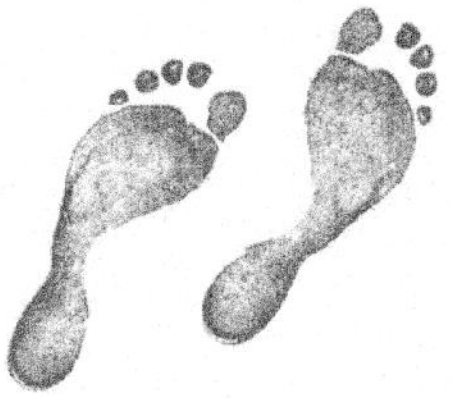

PADA 23
DAWN IN LUZ

I wake very early this morning, still feeling the unwelcome twist of contraction in my gut. It is a little cold this November morning in Luz, Portugal, and still dark as I climb out of bed. I go to the little desk I have dragged over to the window, and sit watching the first pale orange streaks of light emerging from the edge of the Atlantic Ocean. The sea shimmers, liquid silver tinged with fire. The twinkling lights of a few fishing boats float on this awesome, generous dawning sea…

Writing always brings perspective, focus, understanding, integration, rest…

Only Consciousness, only Reality, is always the pre-existing case, in all circumstances, under all conditions. Unless the bodymind, the instrument of perception, is attuned, is perfectly open to taste the true nature of this Reality that we are, we miss. We miss the point, we miss the mark. (*Missing the mark* is the old translation of the word *sin*.)

Unless all the surface bodies are purified, what we taste is the distortion. How does this purification take place? By simple persistent observation and an ever-increasing, unresisting, willing, loving embrace of the current experience, the present taste of life in the moment. The awareness of this simplicity brings about a draining, a continual emptying out of self, of ownership. This can feel like intense depression or deprivation as everything the little personality had longed for, and appeared to own, is removed piece by piece, is allowed to dissolve.

This is a continual experience of heartbreaking dying to individual possession, to attachment, to ownership, to any personal desire which is linked to an idea of the possibility of loss or guilt or fear, anything which is not just simple expression. The removal of any lingering longing is an experience of ripping away, like old sticking plaster being torn from the tender skin to which it is adhering!

All this is simply experience, which the play of the *gunas*, Sanskrit for the three qualities of nature, and the so-called karmic destiny, is creating. My Home, my body, are emotional experiences, when the idea of personal ownership pervades them, like a spider's web. Everything is given; nothing is to be clung to. Everything is so temporary. Aching death and exquisite rebirth in every moment.

The current of reality flows into the five rivers of the senses. The conditioning of the conscious and unconscious mind creates the play of life, the game of Maya, for the enjoyment of Being. The instrument witnesses this. Being enjoys the show, and the apparent individual fragment of consciousness gradually penetrates the illusion of time and space. Everything that this seeming individual possesses will dissolve anyway within time. As Kabir says, better to cut your ropes willingly while still breathing, as you will never do this when the physical body has dropped without your conscious consent.

Jeanette is in the unrelenting grip of Rahu, who is tenderly stripping her of the veils of illusion. Everything will be given and everything taken. Her life is a crash course in the purest form of realisation. This is her chosen destiny. **Only this is Real**. Anything less will never satisfy her. Life always uses the most personal intimate desires to fulfil its purpose. When she no longer has any emotional attachment to a home, when the experience of lack is of less importance than a mosquito bite, then this gift will simply and naturally be given.

Now I understand the purpose of the experience of being kicked out of the room I was staying in!

When a place in which to be in this world is a natural unfolding, then the contraction, the emotional recoil on the self, which prevents anything from simply flowing into form, is dissolved. I see how the individual consciousness prevents the events we most desire from unfolding. This transcendence of the last shreds of emotional attachment, and fear of so-called loss, is to be learnt first. We prevent what is natural from unfolding!

Jeanette absolutely has to first learn to accept being a wanderer forever! When I am happily willing to be 'homeless' forever, then I can have a home! I keep myself from Paradise, as most do when any shred of emotional attachment remains. It must all be dissolved, a weed which is untrue, rooted in fear and unreality.

As the *Avadhuta Gita* says,*"My form has been dissolved, I am free from disease."*

In perceiving the truth, peace descends again. The sun is well risen, high in the sky. A path of light blazes across the sea to touch my balcony, blinding me, making it hard to see the screen of my laptop. My bare feet are chilled on the cold tiled floor and I begin to feel autumnal, even here in Portugal.

Maybe I will get the landlady to light the wood burner in the living room this evening. The family in the apartment below left for the airport in the early morning, long ago. It is time to make hot tea, to bathe this body and continue the process of dying today. Let us see what the new day brings.

Praia da Luz, Portugal, 2 November 2003

PADA 24
THE WOMB WALL

Our experience of this cosmic display that we call our life is completely dependent upon our inner landscape. This landscape is a shifting sand of mountains and valleys, oceans and rivers, chasms and forests as in the outer world, all formed from the fallout patterns of our first experience of light and sound, at the fusion of the first two cells.

It is truly a pattern of drifting particles, which we attempt to assemble into some semblance of coherence. The knowing of our nature as consciousness is retained as a faint echo, growing ever more distant as we identify with the reflection all around us, mirrored to us by the circumstances in which we appear to find ourselves. We begin to believe, as in a nightmare, that we are what is mirrored to us, as a swan among ducklings is imprinted with ducklingness. The echo becomes fainter and fainter in our experience as consciousness is imprinted with the ways of being of our parents, ancestors of the body and society.

"O the mind has mountains, cliffs of fall, frightful sheer no-man-fathomed. Hold them cheap, May who ne'er hung there." - Gerard Manley Hopkins

Our individual experience of the cosmic mandala is entirely unique. Our exit from this dimension is often experienced as the tunnel of light as we leave this dream by 'death'.

We have the destiny to wake up from the distortion, the nightmare, while still apparently within the cosmic display in the flesh, when we attend to that faint echo of knowing, and amplify that by our attention, until it replaces the distortion.

Occasionally, an individual entity awakens to realise this spontaneously. Traditionally in religious and 'spiritual' life, we can harmonise under the umbrella of a teacher-saviour-master, and experience the matrix through 'their doorway'.

We are, however, called to true autonomy, when we are no longer carried by any form. The cracks in this womblike landscape are appearing as we put our baby fists through the walls of belief, which have kept us in our box.

Like the alchemist, we are beginning to stick our heads through the roof of the worlds, and feel both our joy at the vision of freedom, and our sorrow at the loss of our toys, and the absence of the vision of the myriad stars as they used to appear to us.

20 June 2006

PADA 25
THE REAL

From early childhood I was drawn in my awareness to the Real. As I knew it then, it was in the person of Jesus. I began to love Reality and to know that vibration of the Heart. I loved to be in quiet places. In an empty church, in nature, lying in the long grass in the field behind my house. They called me a day-dreamer. I was simply attending to the Real. I also loved stories, and read voraciously!

At fourteen I had a direct cognition of the nature of Reality. I knew, without process, no difference between the body of Christ as the Communion wafer, and the red plastic of the seat where I was sitting upstairs on a Leicester double decker bus. I was a devout child. It turned my world inside out.

It took years for the inner and outer aspects of my knowing to become one, and for me to accept the absolute validity of this knowledge. No one else in my world seemed to know, and yet it was unquestionably true. I searched through Christian mysticism and eastern gurus, and the radical simplicity of this knowledge deepened until it was completely obvious to me that what I am is the same as Reality, indeed Reality Itself. There is no other. There is nothing else to know. Simply to embrace the story that we are with curiosity, and to live that to the full, in the knowledge or ignorance of our nature. It makes no difference.

The simplicity of Being shines as everything. It has no preference. Awake or asleep, shallow or profound, resisting or embracing all, judged by mind or not, there is simply Being. This awareness can bring acceptance and peace to the apparent individual, but Being is not concerned. The sun shines on all indifferently.

My old mind became like a leaky sieve, full of holes. Realisation gave rise to different states, and many wild, and sometimes terrifying, experiences. Sometimes bliss, sometimes temporarily destabilised. The magnetic pull of Being drawing attention inwards, created the desire to go live in a cave or a convent, as the Heart fell into the absolute. Desiring to simply **be** this truth, and leave all story behind. But whatever unfolded, caves and monasteries or abandoned living, fear or radiance, pain or bliss, it was still the story unfolding!

Eventually attention stabilised on what it loves, and began to learn the secret of how to live resting in the Heart, giving attention to the Real throughout all changing states of mind, body and emotion. I became delighted with the ordinariness of the story, learning painfully slowly, by direct experience, that whatever state Jeanette seemed to be in, nothing changed in awareness. Only the living radiance is Real, and unaffected by the story.

This 'practice' can bring peace. But conditional life is continually in flux, experience fluctuates and conditioned being finds the practice hard. Attention is drawn to the changing storyline, and believes this is Real. However, in chaos or stillness, weeping or laughing, blind or enlightened, Being shines in all its movies. Nothing needs to change for Being. There is no other. Enlightenment is not the issue here. Whether enjoying or suffering in your story, Being simply **is**.

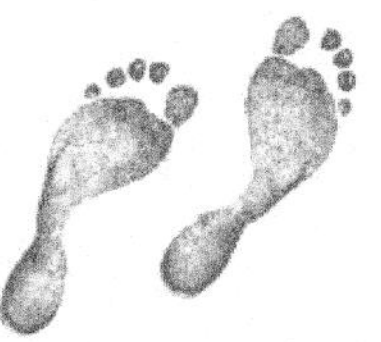

PADA 26
THE BALLET HOO

I watched the Ballet Hoo giving a stage performance of the Romeo and Juliet ballet they have been rehearsing for the last 18 months. I have also been watching the rehearsals on television these last weeks. The performance was magnificent. Rich costumes, awesome choreography, and the **feeling**.

You would not believe that these dancers were novices. Except for the tears of their mentors and directors in the audience. The feeling of awe and love in the transformation of these rebellious, dropout, streetwise kids into magical performers was amazing. And prophetic for me. Tybalt's swordfight and death were stunning. The young black rebel who played Tybalt is amazing. I am in love with his freedom, and the beauty of the way his body moves as he dances and fights. I was fighting with him, in short doses though.

I want to stabilise in that place of simply loving that movement. It is this feeling, this pristine focus. They integrated some fantastic breakdancing into the ballet, and choreographed it with the same precision. The teenagers were transfigured by this acceptance, and magic shone from the whole venture. They just loved that their breakdancing was included, and it was brilliant.

Strictly Come Dancing was on the other channel. Again the feeling of transformation, and loving the freedom of the movement. But there was not the *flow* of feeling in the Heart, as with the young dancers of the Ballet Hoo emerging from the shadow, learning about dedication, and commitment, and surrender, and togetherness, and performance, and love. It is this enormous flow in the Heart that is so Real.

Even as I am drowning…

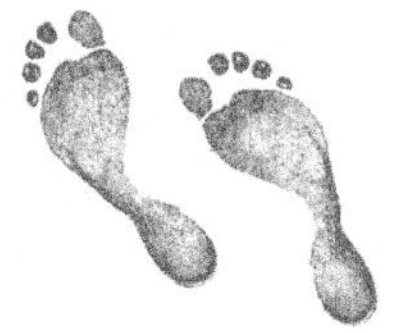

PADA 27
IT'S ALL ME

Then talking with my friend the next day, he was doing some telepathic journey in the body that I didn't quite see. He tells me to put my finger or two fingers left of the navel, and then here and there. He is seeing something, but when I don't viscerally see it, it's not yet useful to me.

I know it is all embodied. Fasting, breathing, feeling as the Heart, whatever attention is drawn to, unwinding movement which is fun and spontaneous with feeling in the Heart, Heart Communication, all of these shift the coordinates.

I see, like the Rishis, that we are literally able to take responsibility for anything in our lives. This is precision creation. Our destiny. To see how we each create the crazy dreamlike circumstances of our life, making a kind of jumbled sense, like a dream. To see how thoughts are refracted through the prism of this bodymind, creating the circumstances around Jeanette.

It all just happens. Awareness dawns. There is an exquisite implicate order in the chaos. We can simply examine every event, every breath, in the structure of the surface bodies, and dissolve it all into the Heart. The unintegrated shadow relentlessly draws congealed flow into form. No controlling or strategy.

I must move as softly as water poured out, or I create further resistance and contraction.

Friday 29 September

PADA 28
NOTHING TO DO

This morning I begin the rejuvenation process promised last year by my friend, who has made me wait days longer than it seems necessary to me. As a result of my experiences of last week, I walk to his hut at 7.45 this morning empty, with no sense of anticipation. This is just some appointment we agreed on a long time ago, and now the day has arrived. All personal desire for this process has died, and right now, I am indifferent about the outcome, or even whether we do it.

Arun asks how I am. "Body, mind or Heart?" I smile wryly.

"All." He looks at me. "You."

I don't tell him how emptied I am. How emotionless.

"I'm okay. What to do?" I say in my best Kerala accent, waggling my head from side to side, South Indian style.

"Nothing to do," he replies. "Just wait and see."

I am drawn to tell him one of my favourite Sufi stories, about the old man, his son and the horse.

"There was once a very old man who lived in a far-off country. He was very poor, and his only possession was a beautiful mare that lived in a stable next to the poor cottage, where the old man lived with his only son.

One day the boy, being a little careless, left the stable door open, and the mare escaped and ran off into the hills.

As in the village everyone's life is an open book, the neighbours, enjoying the drama, came round to commiserate. "Oh you poor old man. This horse was your only possession. Now what will you do in your old age. What a terrible misfortune."

All the old man would say was, "Who knows? Let's just wait and see."

The next day the mare came back, bringing six wild stallions with her, and the son quickly shut them in the stable. As usual the neighbours came round to comment. "How amazing. Now you will be rich. What wonderful luck!"

The old man said nothing except, "Who knows? Let's just wait and see."

The next day the son began breaking in one of the horses. He fell off and broke his leg in several places, very badly.

The neighbours came round again. "Oh you poor old man. Maybe your son will never walk again. Now what will you do? Who is going to look after you in your old age? What a misfortune."

The old man again said nothing but "Who knows? Let's just wait and see."

The following week the neighbouring country declared war, and the king called all the young men in the kingdom into the army to fight for their country.

Well there was such weeping and wailing, and the neighbours came to see the old man again. "You were right, old man. Now we have lost our sons, and yours is still alive to keep you company, at least."

But the old man would say only, "Let's just say that your sons have been taken and mine has been left, and who knows what will come of this."

Arun looks at me.

"One thing you can be sure of, everything changes in every moment."

We go inside and I take off my clothes.

"First sit here."

I sit on the stool and he works on my head, neck and shoulders, pouring half a cup of thick, green, sweet-smelling oil onto the crown of my head.

My impression of Arun swings regularly between an inspired master, and a sullen Kerala boy! It's probably all my projection, or maybe both are true.

The massage is good, and he uses the true tantric regeneration techniques, completely impersonally. I am amazed at the lack of pain, as last year I was regularly covered in bruises from his treatment. I cannot tell whether the tension in my body has diminished, or if he's being gentler. Both I suppose. I tell him it is not hurting. He says, "Your body is better. Do you want me to hurt you?" I say, "No no!" hastily, but then I wonder at the thought, and again at the complexity of his personality, and the impossibility of real communication with him. Last year I was still integrating the shadow of abuse. This year it's different.

Lying on his table, I contemplate the pale sky and the ever-present Kerala coconut palms, visible through the triangular opening in the roof of his hut, realising once again the infinitely merciful, seamless flow of life, which has brought me to this indescribable state of indifference, before beginning this process.

"Nothing to do, nowhere to go."

Kerala, Thursday 3 May 2001

PADA 29
CONNECTION

This morning I walked to the internet office near the beach. Andres is sitting at a computer, checking his email. I sit in the seat beside him.

"How are you Purnima?" he asks.

"My heart is broken and it's ok and I'm smiling," I say quietly. "I'm dying. What else to do? *Asi es la vida*!"

"And you're not resisting it," he says very gently. "I was coming to see you after this, but now you are here." I look into the spaciousness in his eyes. The tears well up irresistibly from my Heart, and I feel my eyes fill.

"It's such a blessing to be with people who are in this space of emptiness."

"Oh! Oh Purnima!" He is touched by the same feeling that is moving me. He reaches out and puts his arms round me for a long moment, and the melting deepens.

"Connection!" calls Manu, who runs the email office. He has managed to get us online at last, and we turn to our terminals and start our emails.

Kerala, Thursday 3 May 2001

PADA 30
WAVES

In the late afternoon I walk down to the beach, and sit for a long time in the low waves at the edge of the sea. The fishermen are out in their pointed boats, rowing along parallel to the shore, and four or five girls in bright saris wander by.

The girls look with curiosity, or maybe even envy, at me sitting playing in the sand, the waves lifting my legs and roughly spinning me around as they recede. One wave drains away, revealing three tiny conical shells encircled with alternating bands of cream and brown, half buried in the swirling water beside me.

I sift them out of the wet sand, turning them in my hand, enjoying the soft precision of their markings and their quiet vulnerability. Within the shell, a small, white, protoplasmic being is pulsating, innocently embodied, like a baby. This is my body. This is my blood. This is my life. I let them slip from my hand and they disappear without trace swallowed up by the sea.

I stand and wade out into the water to wash away the sand. Feeling myself a giant, my legs like two great pillars striding through the world of little sea creatures.

A haze of clouds covers the sky and the day is hot again, washed clean after the heavy, pre-monsoon rains and thunder storms of the last few days. Starbursts of grey-green coconut palms wave their fronds, hanging above red cliffs where occasional splashes of brilliant yellow-green vegetation have blossomed. This is a new communion, a new birth. Wherever I look, fresh waves of word pictures roll rhythmically through my mind, with the constant tumbling motion of the sea, and I am impelled back to my room to write.

I take the path bordering the channel of rushing water, which is more than a stream and not quite a river, and I stop to watch two men in patterned lungis hitched up above their knees, standing on stones in the water, scrubbing a patient white goat. The paddy fields I walk through every day are full of these wandering goats, with yellow slit eyes and long swollen udders, dangling like pointed, creamy pink carrots, they graze calmly, dragging the tails of their tethering cords along behind them, like Little Bo Peep's sheep.

Kerala, Thursday 3 May 2001

PADA 31
SPACE

Lying in bed in the early morning, feeling the body breathing, simple, innocent, like little molluscs, I dissolve into the ocean. Everything is breathing itself. The Heart is beating itself. I listen to the waves rhythmically breaking on the shore like a heartbeat, my hand lies on the smooth rounded flesh of my belly, pulsating, rising and falling like the waves in the sea. No separation. Fingers stroke soft silk curve of breast. The body is always entirely innocent. Vulnerable as a baby.

Dwadiumasto govinda. Diupiameva samarpaye.

Your thing, O Lord, we give back to You.

I remember this beautiful grace we used to chant before eating. One of the good things we shared, he used to sit across the table from me in the kitchen, his eyes shining at me, enjoying. The mind, this beautiful intellect, this Buddhi, this lamp at the doorway, can be a thief. Unintegrated Buddhi steals the light of its own existence from the whole. It must know itself as only the Heart. I am a thief to the extent that I see anything as my own possession. When I am truly aware of my nothingness, I have become life itself. I have become everything. This separate mind will do everything it can to prevent real integration, for this is death to itself, to personal ownership – death of little self, body as personal property, mind, money, emotions, right, relationships, everything.

Life is integrating itself in this space. Not **my** space. Its **own** space. There is no me. Life belongs only to itself. There is no other. The idea of loss and betrayal has arisen in this space, only to die. It died because I did not fight it. Finally I was able to welcome it. I know that Lord Buddh will now change his form. The Gemini energy is transforming. Mercury, Buddh, has changed sign. He has moved house from Aries to Taurus, and is now living in Venus' house. He will come less now to visit me. I am grateful now to whoever stole the money from me, the puffed-up parasitic prince of separate ego mind no longer needs to flaunt himself in this form. He can become simple. He has integrated in this one, and the pull is no longer experienced. In another form he was also the carrier for me of this mean energy that believes in limitation. He also is set free to die. This energy of duality is dissolving. These old myths of loss, death and betrayal rise from the depths of the earth to die in the shallows like beached whales, dying with relief in the light of day. Accepted, absolved of guilt, dying in simplicity, returning their energy to the whole.

PADA 32
BASILISK AND OBSIDIAN

Years ago, I dreamt I am standing on a high ledge outside a cave mouth, on the side of a Himalayan mountain, gazing down over a vast plain. As I stand looking, two huge monolithic giants of stone rise from the depths of the earth to visit me. Their names are Basilisk and Obsidian, and they are very ancient.

They are vast, silent, powerful brooding presences, and they could have crushed me in a trice, like an ant. Instead, they acknowledge me solemnly, and I know no fear. Rather, I am their equal. They simply bow to me with dignity, then sink back again into the depths of the earth, to their assigned place.

They are gone. And although at that point in time I have no understanding of their visit, I know my business with them is not finished. Like so many mysterious visions, I ponder this one in silence in my Heart, for to whom do you speak of such events?

I look up their names in encyclopaedias and dictionaries, and discover that Basilisk is a mythical animal, a dragon which hatches from an egg, and has eyes that turn to stone, and Obsidian is a shiny, black, extremely hard volcanic rock, sometimes used in black magic practices. Certainly these were not easy beings to be with, but they were part of me, part of my destiny.

Over these last years, the ancient shadow of the dark, manipulative, controlling, wrathful, unmoving, implacable tamasic feminine, the dark Medusa, the devouring mother, with eyes which turn all to stone, who needs to be controlled or placated, arose from the unconscious. I allowed her energy to live in me, twisting as a whirlwind, distorting this body into a spiral. I gave space, a home, to the Rahu Devi. I let her in.

The dark mother came out of the deep to integrate herself. Now she is dying in me, falling, finally surrendered, head to the ground, innocent, relieved of guilt, freed from the burden of maintaining a separate unreal existence. Her power is gone.

All the old myths are integrating, dying. I often used to ask myself the question why did Ramana Maharshi die? Today I know, and I understand the story of the Heart. All is love, all is one. Ramana's body was the Heart, and everything was welcome to be there. Because of my interest in bodywork I was also interested in the site of Ramana's cancer, as indeed I am curious about the site of any happening in the body, for the body is a playground for Truth.

Ramana had a growth on the elbow of his left arm. In the foetus the tiny arm buds begin to form at the same moment as the heart begins to beat. They are one with the energy of the Heart. The arms are the Heart in expression, and the power to give and receive.

When we consider the left side of the body to be the feminine, the tamasic power, the distillation of the poison of the shadow of the mother, was welcomed into his body. Because he freely allowed the cancer in, this toxic shadow arose from the dark of the unconscious to be visible, to integrate. The poison, which was the shadow of the mother, found a home in Ramana, to be in, and to die in. She came to him because he resisted nothing. He let her in because he welcomed all Beings.

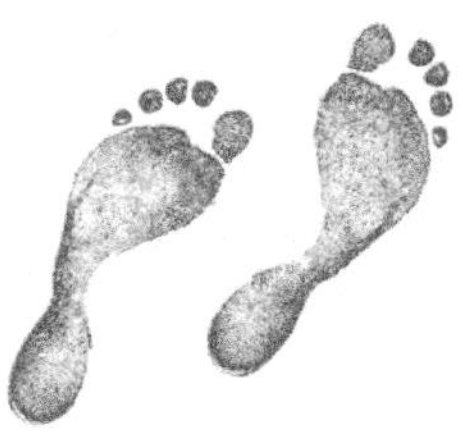

PADA 33
DUSK

At dusk I often walk on the beach. The people gather ritually to watch, to talk, and to enjoy the relatively cool evening air. I walk along the edge of the water, careless of getting my clothes wet. The faintest of breezes comes from the sea.

The colours of the evening sky are indescribable. Drifts of soft purple and lilac and smoky grey clouds, flame and salmon and pink streaks of light float in a sea of luminous turquoise and pale aquamarine sky. Gaps in the clouds let in spaces of brilliant light.

I see this show so often, and it's always breathtakingly fresh. Ribbing, in banks of indigo cloud, looks like patterned sand after the ebbed tide. Wispy shapes of vapour form vast wings across the sky. It reminds me of the Gerald Manley Hopkins poem:

"And for all this, nature is never spent;
There lives the dearest freshness deep down things;
And though the last lights off the black West went
Oh, morning, at the brown brink eastward, springs
Because the Holy Ghost over the bent
World broods with warm breast and ah! bright wings."

This time of day, dusk, is *Sandhya*, the gap, the space between night and day. Like dawn, it's a magical time, when the rhythm of the day is ceasing, and the rhythm of the night is not yet established, and more can squeeze through cracks in the mind.

I sit cross-legged on the sand, watching and listening to the waves, until the sea turns silver and white, and first Venus and little points of light appear, one after another, in the darkening sky. The moon is almost full this evening, and I reach up and touch her face.

Om sri somaye namaha.
Greetings Oh Great Being of Bliss.

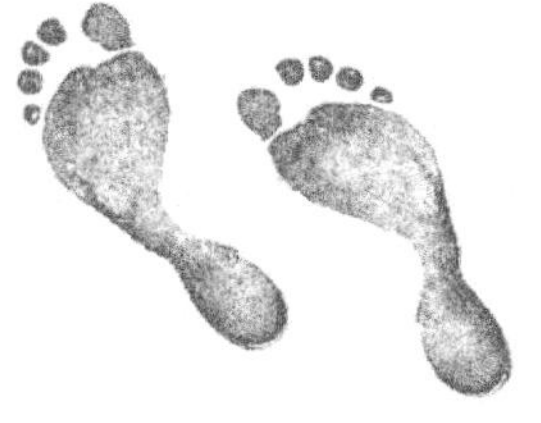

PADA 34
TREASURE

Human beings have the potential to become full spectrum beings expressing their potential in an endless variety of ways.

Conditioning by the environment, upbringing, education, our given genetic inheritance, our imprint at conception and birth, form the reflection we receive in the mirror of our environment, shaping our beliefs.

Feedback from the environment further defines our expression, showing us what is acceptable, what is approved of, defining what we can do and are good at, ultimately what we seem to become.

A construct of what we are and can become is created, narrowing the spectrum, the ways in which we choose to live and express what we are. In this fashion our mind, our body, our relationships, our circumstances are continually defined by reference to the external picture of what seems to be possible.

This tiny bubble of what is seen creates, defines and limits our narrow spectrum individual expression and experience of our world. Our womb. To step outside this framework takes vision, courage, a willingness to allow the walls of the womblike view of what seems to be 'your' life, to dissolve, a willingness to begin to contemplate a fuller spectrum existence, to include other means than the conscious thinking mind of contemplating it all.

Our life, our universe, has a fractaline nature. It can open, expand and flower wherever attention rests. The flow of neutral attention is a powerful instruction to the mind that this is what we value, what we love.

"For where your treasure is, your heart will be also."
– Matthew 6:21

14 March 2003

PADA 35
GATEWAYS

Look at the pictures in front of your eyes with soft eyes, whether they are objects, events or desires of your own illusory ego. Do not desire anything to be different. All is as it is. All is God. Even the patterns of your ego are to be seen softly. Soften and watch. Soften your gaze. Hard eyes sharpen the edges and produce resistance, solidity, emotion.

E-motion moves you out of your centre, which is the only place you can truly see from. Do not be moved from your centre, meaning do not even imagine that you can be moved from your centre.

You are Reality looking at Itself. You have become conscious as Yourself in order to simply see Yourself.

I have no beginning and no end. I pass through many gateways. Many eyes are My Gateways. I need your eyes, My Own Eyes, to see Myself. I wish My Eyes to be conscious as Myself. How can the unconscious eye see itself?

It must know what It is. Your eye is My Own Form. I wish My Eye to see and to Know Me. I wish to know Myself. You are My Own Form, My Son, My Daughter.

You are all rays of pure light, perfect in every sense. Remember, everything, every event, is an open door to Truth with soft eyes, or a closed door when seen with hard eyes. Open the door and look through the doorway. Everything Is. Listen through the sound. Your brother is you, is God Himself. This is the absolute Truth, and utterly obvious. He could not exist if he were not. His voice is the sound of God. Like this computer, but only the froth on the surface, a footprint. Look and listen through the gaps.

Only God is. His manifest form is empty, infinitely, intricately, enfolded within Itself. All exists - without qualification. Just look and fall in love with Yourself. Watch the surface change and dissolve, like jewelled cobwebs in the sun, while in reality nothing happens. In the Heart is unmoving, unending, changeless peace.

Only Happiness Is.

PADA 36
ALICE

I have such an ache in my pelvis, aching all over now. And depressed.

And unable to do postures, with no pull to do anything because of no flow. My energy is all screwed up. Backache, everything hurts.

The Yoga welcome pack came, and I feel so useless that it seems to have nothing to do with me. I just made an energy jam into something worse. Can I really contemplate this? Must be out of my mind.

So, I go in my attention to my place where there is nothing to do, complete coherence always, how I have lived all these years.

I come to my bed and let it be.

I curl up very very small, like Alice in Wonderland, in the Heart, and lay my mind and body down and rest in the chaos, in Crazyland. In a while I will sleep, slip back into the deep.

I practise paradoxical intention. Let it be total chaos. I merge with it and match it, and it is then ok for it to be as it is, helplessness, with no change ever. I do not need to improve anything.

In this place there is no Yoga, no teacher, no *Kapalbhati* breathing, no Jeanette, no pain, no problem.

I can't do anything since I am non-doing, nothing.

Who is this 'I' who is helpless and in pain?

At first there are tears as I feel my helplessness, and I let it be and stop attempting to make it better, and then it gets quieter...

It is Rumi's field... out beyond ways of wrong and right doing. No *yamas* or *niyamas*. No mistakes. Nothing to heal.

I will see tomorrow if there is anything of any importance left...

Wednesday evening, 3rd July

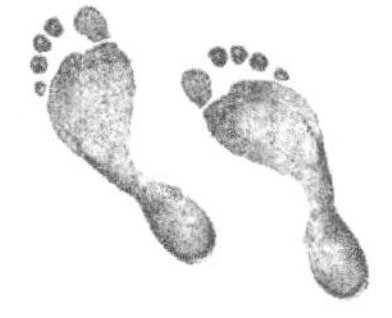

PADA 37
OUR LITTLE SNOW GLOBE

The petals of the stars open. Light flowers.
"Baby eye perceiving dot-by-dot the matrix of infinity."

Star children falling like snowflakes, thickly carpeting the mountain.

At the end of the pantomime Little Red Riding Hood and the Wolf stand hand-in-hand, and take their bow together.

This whole world, this little snow globe, this bubble of space-time is you outpictured. You in expression. Everything is simply consciousness. Experienced as Heaven when the mind and Heart are in union. Or Hell when mind is divorced from its root in the Heart.

As a baby all is one. Then the All becomes differentiated. This offers a way to experience Yoga, union. By choice in the moment. As a HeartField. In Keyala.

With a simple shift in perception, stabilised and embodied, you can experience chaos and conflict, or Yoga and grace.

PADA 38
BABY JANE

Autumn 1988

The Real and the unreal.
The volcano erupts! There is no volcano.

My body suddenly erupts into a roaring volcano. It has been brewing for a couple of days, since a bodywork session a few days ago. It feels like an energy-inflated balloon, the skin of my energy field stretched to bursting. And then a sudden spontaneous eruption. I become a raging sea of hot lava. Alternating bliss and excruciating pain.

Terror, and zero understanding of what is happening.

I am doing Yoga and breathing in the meditation room. I get up and run from the room. As if I could escape from this irrevocably changed body. Since then I have lived with this for more than 34 dysfunctional years.

Later that evening I sit on the floor and violently draw massive spirals with a thick red wax crayon…

Then write all over it, describing what had happened. I have the huge sheet of paper from my flip chart in front of me now as I copy the words. How it feels to allow this power and rage to emerge!

Sitting on the floor in the empty Yoga hall I begin to write.

10.40 pm, Thursday 17th November 1988

I am writing down how it felt to do this drawing as suggested, in case I forget by next week.

I draw the red spirals first, and then the purple violet rays streaming up from the base. Then the golden loops of light which came after the first penetration of the spine had reached my head. The amazing radiance which filled me felt like that. Then the streaks of black are the pain with which I feel my spine and womb are being penetrated. Not always, as at times there is an incredible gentleness and sweetness. Then I want to emphasise the red spirals, and I draw them more violently this time. More and more violently, and then I scream. Four, five times, and frighten myself with the violence, and then I try it again when I get used to the idea! Then I draw the central red core. That's what it feels like after a time. That I am just being opened up. This feels so masochistic. I feel myself growling and snarling like a caged animal, a wild animal. So I tried growling a bit more and terrify myself with the sound, and so have a glass of wine. Feeling a bit drunk by now, I go to make a piece of toast and Marmite, and scream a few more times. I've done all this before. I've looked at rage and my repressed shadow.

Will I never be free? The energy is still freaking me. Now I start to cry. I want someone to help me. I want someone here. But there is no one, only me. I scream again. I feel drunk, and now I really cry, and only my need to make sense of this later makes me keep writing down what is happening. I can't really trust anything. I have to watch for myself. The life force doesn't love me. It has a will of its own, but I want to feel loved. I want someone to love me. I want to go home. It is hard, determined. It feels like I experienced my mother. Cold, impersonal, uncaring at the moment.

"Relentless, implacable." Since then I have come to live with what I have much later come to know intimately as my Beloved Opponent.

I scream again and start to cough. Illegible words now…

I'm killing it with the rage there is in me.

I scribble all over this writing with my red wax crayon. Having scribbled all over my writing I feel a bit calmer. We shall have something to talk about next week. Ha! I have a sore throat. It's all still there. Not quite so strong, I'm going to bed now. Such violence in me. I remember talking about anger. It struck me. I am obviously not finished with this yet!

Thoughts in present time 2022 as I re-read and transcribe this piece, and re-live the event

Later, researching parallels for my life-changing experience, I read some texts on kundalini. While there are some similarities, there are also many differences.

I recall the sense of being "cribbed, cabined and confined". Trussed like a stuffed dummy, for surgeries. And more. Screamed, but been unheard, invaded, controlled and abused. Force fed, my will twisted as a child. Confused, I learnt to follow the crucified Christ. And then to have to walk away from him, or the construct, or projection. Realising the unreality of experience. I made it ALL up!

A house divided cannot stand. But Here I AM! Still!

A lifetime of becoming aware of, and integrating, these energies and illusions. And not actually going mad! Learning to keep my own counsel. Closing the gap between experience and knowing. Setting myself free. See my poem *Shadow Baby*, Baby Jane in conjunction with this story (at the beginning of this book). An anthology is being published soon with a selection of more of my poetry, exploring embodiment and realisation beyond control, and the patterns of robotic automaticity. *"Realising drop by drop the matrix of Infinity."*

I have more to say elsewhere about all this, and polishing our gift of Choice. And going the long way round to see through it all.

There is no other!

PADA 39
UGLY DUCKLINGNESS

There is a lot of hype about enlightenment. It appears to be a mysterious exalted state. Our freedom, bliss and power, and those who have assigned themselves the frequency of seekers, and play that part for now in the drama of life, remain constantly on that 'spiritual path'. Wilful pursuit of this 'high State' implies that we do not know that state of oneness with the ocean of life in which we inhere, that we are ignorant of our true nature. Our natural state, into which we are born. The fact that the minds of others around us seem unaware of that state of bliss renders them, for the most part, unable to reflect more than a trickle of our inheritance to us. Our mind imprints with ugly ducklingness, and we forget our true nature, our true authority.

We become imprinted with concepts of hard work, struggle, control, pain, lack, fear, guilt, regret, unworthiness. competition and more. Even if we rebel against these, as aspects of us do, there is resistance, inertia, rebellion and rage instead. Our inheritance, our natural flow or energy to follow our impulse, and the connection with our sovereign authority, seems lost. We become thirsty as Osho says, like fish in the ocean looking for water.

Discussions and conferences about enlightenment, which is a self-evident fact, emphasises this state of separation in which mind appears to exist. The state of alienation of the mind from what IS grows greater as mind focuses on 'how to'. The fog becomes denser, and the unhappy fish swim about in schools discussing how to get back to the ocean. Life is drawn into form for pleasure and joy, rather than discussion. If we want to serve humanity, we can serve the process of life itself - and ourselves - by falling back into the natural state of simplicity and bliss, and radiating this. We serve best by becoming Real. Flowering in what might seem to be a desert. Swans swimming in the midst of those who play the ugly duckling game.

It's so simple. Open your eyes and look around. We exist in heaven. What we are never left. It's all a mind game. What you put attention on grows. The way you see it grows. And if you don't see it the way you like, begin to choose differently. The kingdom of heaven is all around you. Choose to notice it, and it reveals itself to you.

It is in the tiny everyday things we have to begin to activate our pre-existing freedom. Step-by-step, breath by breath. Heart already knows, and boldly carries that imprinted memory of that moment of a nuclear fusion of conception. Each cell vibrating with that piezo electric spark. Mind was not designed for struggling to understand. The mind is a focusing tool for the Heart. To facilitate the expression of desire. Desire... *de sidere,* meaning 'from the stars'.

We are embodied packets of desire, light, information, pleasure delight. Allow mind to fall into the Heart, abandoning this state of fragmentation, into that flow of joy, that well of living water springing up into eternal life. In this natural state it is not a question of working out how to attract what we need. It rises naturally, created as we allow scattering of the seeds of our desire in this garden.

It can be a desert or Paradise Garden, as we choose to see it. Life is for living and abundantly celebrating enjoying, not discussing how!

9 June 2011

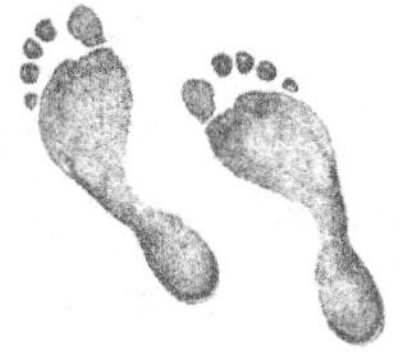

PADA 40
WILD DEPRESSION

I wake this morning without the feeling of dread. Though very regressed. The house is the biggest tip ever. I no longer pick anything up. I don't know where anything is. The fridge smells like a dead rat is in there. I am like a little animal in its burrow. I am a wild creature. I don't care about being civilised. No one can see you anyway. I am living some weird disconnected life.

I speak with clients on the phone, and that part of me does an excellent job, fully present, magnificent. But in this house I am losing it - chaos - I can't find anything. But I don't care. I go without whatever it is I wanted to find. How long before the finances get into a real muddle?

Next week the cleaning lady comes. I guess I might create some kind of order for her. I am in a deep depression, but not all of me is there. I am still writing. Some parts of me are still functioning, and today there is no dread. Just apathy. I am like a caged wild animal that has deteriorated from lack of freedom. I could sing, or make sounds, or jump on my rebounder. I make occasional trips to the kitchen for water or food, which I simply take like a child left locked up. It is all in a heap everywhere. I'm reminded of some of Ronnie Laing's stories I read maybe 30 years ago. I am regressing. I don't know who to talk to.

I am a little wild animal. She doesn't care about order. I don't care about anything much, except sitting here and writing in the dark. I play patience for hours, and look at the trees. Occasionally I get the urge to do something, and I write. I should sell this house and move. But where to?

How is it I can function at all? I do not know how to look after her. We are trapped here. I just see how dysfunctional I am becoming, and yet I have to be here for her. I do not know how to help her, or at all what she wants. I want to dispose of all this stuff, but it takes thought and planning to do that.

The thought comes she might like the Zen theatre next week. I can't open the flyer online. If nothing matters then I will just live from day-to-day for a while. There is enough money for a few months. Maybe something will resolve. Maybe I can just be, and allow it all to unravel. I have to go to Ireland in July. I have to do things like book tickets, buy clothes. I can just be here at least for a few days, and see what evolves. There has to be a whole new way of living, and I don't know how to get there. I am too little to manage to know what I want, and how to live in this unreal world. I want to run wild and live out in the woods, simple, with very little. I do not know how to restore my body to a state where I can be fit enough to get out of this place with all its stuff. I don't even go out into the garden now. I caught sight of the giant poppies yesterday on the way into the house. My father loved them. Maybe I could go and look at them a bit later. Maybe I could wash the dishes. Maybe pack up some clothes. Maybe clean the fridge.

I am despondent about living a life like this. I was free before I came back from India, and now I am trapped here. We all have to work together, all the aspects of ourselves, to get ourselves out of this. We have to work together to create a place that we can leave safely when we want to go away. And become fit enough to walk and live in the wild.

We have to look after Baby Jane so she doesn't go crazy, and drag us all down. We are a weird tribe, and we can pull together to escape. We have to undo this crazy life, and simply dispose of all this stuff too. To juggle being here. I'm a wild animal. I sit here naked, but it is cold. I am a wild tribe, and I am the chairman. I have to take care of them. I have to take care of it all. I will begin to empty some of the spaces in this house. For living wild we can begin to start eating. We are a wild tribe. I will begin to assemble us all and see what we can dream, or it will be THE END for all of us

PADA 41
WINTER IN SYCAMORE CLOSE

Life in Sycamore Close is banal and riveting, heartbreaking and totally ordinary. My father is dying of lymphoma, cancer in his blood. He is slowly fading. My mother cares for him like a baby.

I watch them both with an increasing attention, and surprise myself by the quiet pleasure I derive from simply being here, absorbing the experience like a sponge.

For the last two days a couple, a man and a woman, have been pruning the overgrown hedges and trees, and preparing the garden for winter. My mother stands watching. Then this morning as the man cut down a tree which was blocking the growth of other trees, "That's right", she says, talking to herself. "Be careful of my Mahonia Japonica".

"Beautiful yellow flowers in the spring," she says in an aside to me. "In two years' time those red berries…" She stops.

"In two years I won't be here," she says, matter of fact, and no sign of regret.

"I don't want to do any more gardening." She carries on looking.

"What I'm most interested in is that little…" some Latin name. "You see that yellow triangle shape over there? It nearly died, and it should be as big as that plant next to it. I watered it and loved it, and it survived. I thought it was gone."

She looks out of the kitchen window at her garden. "I don't want to do any more gardening now."

I feel the enormity of her love and her care. She has poured it on these plants and on all her gardens, and feel a wave of loving attention, the drops of these present moments being reabsorbed by this still presence, accepting the dissolution of her service to this world. My Heart simply watches in silence. I am here giving total attention to the consuming of this life.

In the afternoon my father comes downstairs for a few moments to be in the kitchen for a while. Bored of lying in bed, and missing my mother, who came down to make a cake. He sits on the hard stool at the kitchen table and tells us about the book he is listening to, one of the audiotapes I brought for him this morning from the library.

He is listening to Graham Greene's *Monsignor Quixote*. For once he is a little animated and tells us a story of priests and housekeepers and cars and bishops.

I watch him with total attention, delighted by his story, clearly seeing and enjoying the Being behind the fragile ageing man, love spontaneously pouring from my Heart. I am in love with how he is. He feels this and tells me the whole story of the car and the petrol and the Bishop, and I am truly entertained. My father was always at his best telling stories.

Afterwards I am suffused by the deepest depression. I am dying. My Being is simply consuming everything.

I call my old friend Barry and weep and weep. I cannot really say why. It is so intense here. Everything falls into the ocean of the moment. I tried to explain the quality of being here, and fail miserably. Barry offers to help me buy a car, and I accept his offer.

At 9 o'clock I go into their bedroom to kiss them goodnight. Like little children they lift up their faces for my kiss. My mother is doing a book of crosswords, and she asks me a word. I give her the answer and sit down to help them finish. We have such a sweet time together laughing, and I get a lot of the answers to the clues. They are so pleased that I get them right. Enjoying the answers and delighted with my clever brain. So sweet.

My mother loves to cook and leaves the kitchen in a mess after every meal. Now I am behaving like her kitchen fairy, enjoying magically cleaning it for her for when she comes down to make something to tempt my father.

My attention on them and this story is vast and silent like the ocean, delighting in and tasting everything. Every moment falling immediately back into the ocean of bliss. Consuming everything.

December 2002

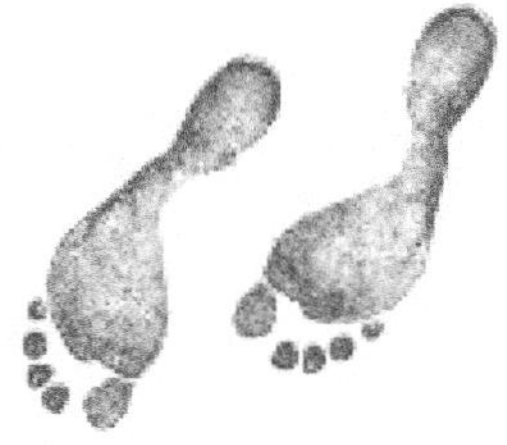

PADA 42
A HOUSE DIVIDED

Shadow is the unknown, not simply discomfort or terror. Resistance to including the more of who each one of us is, both conscious and unconscious. It doesn't feel safe, so we avoid exploring the unknown, beyond the frontiers of our acknowledged space, beyond the boundaries of who we believe ourselves to be, in many ways.

We project aspects of our self onto 'others', our power, our abundance, our qualities and gifts. We give away our perceived weaknesses, our rage, our faults and failings. All this is some hidden power, in the face of which we experience helplessness, the cause of which is as yet invisible, unrecognised. A mysteriousness not yet in full consciousness, a shadowy, and relentless force.

As Carl Jung declares, we are robotically controlled by this congealed force, unless or until we bring it into awareness. "*Man, if indeed thou knowest what thou doest, thou art blessed: but if thou knowest not, thou art cursed, and a transgressor of the law*" - Luke 6:4

I realised I was to inquire into everything I did not completely see the source of, everything which puzzled me. I realised that what I was transmitting, knowingly or unknowingly, I was also receiving. I began to realise all this. To allow the fullness of what 'I Am' to embody, creator, consumer and destroyer of all experience. Integrating, owning that we do not know, our shadow, is uncomfortable, daunting, but suffering is not inevitable. Integration of the unknown and withdrawal of projection is the means of realisation and empowerment, which is the purpose and destiny of all Beings, to discover the Source that I Am. So it is well to welcome the mystery with joy!

"We shall not cease from exploration, and the end of all our exploring will be to arrive where we started and know the place for the first time." - T S Eliot

Shadow denied, not willingly embraced and investigated, is as if saying I see, yet, at the same time, wilfully remaining blind! When embraced with curiosity, the more severe potential effects of living blind can be mitigated. Lack of coherence in self, or wherever experienced, draws us to investigate and acknowledge. This is the Beloved seeking recognition. When recognised, the automaticity of self-attack is dissolved. Accepting our vulnerability is our greatest strength. This is what Jane led me to, living in this way. We cannot live as a house divided. We can live dancing on the razor's edge.

13 August 2019

PADA 43
RAHU IS KEY

Authentic life is before and beyond space-time. It is eternal because it knows no time.

We seem to be collapsing time. At least exploring what time is. Mind using our scientific approach is still rather like ants crawling. Only the mind that surrenders individual ownership can see with the eyes of the one Heart. The eye of authentic love.

Embracing the shadow, the apparently unwanted, is the doorway, which has been locked for aeons. Opening to include the experience of hell, to be curious about the dark, is to unlock the door of egoic experience which binds us in duality. Making the smallest difference between good and bad, pleasure and pain, individual preference, and we are bound in personal time.

"Rahu is the key to eternal life". And in this body I have loved him as my lover. That *"lover beyond compare who dares all for the sake of truth"*. I have seen our luminous completed Earth, and held her in my hands. My child, a living pulsating mass of pure light, and offered her through this triangular opening in the space, created by the swords of three flaming seraphim, into the next dimension.

PADA 44
KRISHNA

My beloved shines all blue today
A sweetly tender pied piper
Softly seducing the stumbling cavalcade
Of shyly tongue-tied children
Limping patterns of lameness
Blind and widely golden eyed

Words of wild strawberries for the mind
Flowing flowering from his fragrant mouth
Innocence clearly calling
Dearly drawing me
Deliciously
Into freefalling radiant darkness
Under the hill of the Heart

Kishori Jeanette McKenzie
Canada, New Year 2000

PADA 45
HELL

My thoughts are images that I have made. The world is a grey triangular barbed wire platform. The world is a concentration camp. The world is hell.

Help!

Who am I asking? Who can help, and who needs or wants help? Who is there who exists anyway?

I had an appointment with the doctor. Now he is supposed to help! The appointment was for 11.15 this morning and the car wouldn't start. This creature that has been called Jeanette since it appeared in this confused kaleidoscopic hell, had an appointment with the doctor, and when the car wouldn't start she cried. It cried!

Now the AA roadside assistance is coming to help! Shall I ask them to fix Jeanette? I think Jeanette is finished for now. Time to give up? Maybe the AA will help to finish her off.

She seems to exist in a flat two-dimensional prison, a vast triangular shield defending her from what lies beyond. A sentry stands on guard duty at each of the three corners of this monotonous grey expanse, with grid-like bars tightly packed with barbed wire, named 'thinking', 'seeing', 'speaking'. A brain, an eye and a tongue. Each emitting a powerful forcefield, reinforcing the power of the other, the beliefs of the brain strengthening the perception of the eye, influencing the language of the tongue, strengthening the beliefs of the brain, an ugly grey pulsating mass, threads of matter connecting it to eye and tongue. Eye seeing grey barren hopelessness and despair, tongue telling endlessly, unreflectingly, unthinkingly, of the bleak vision in the language defined by the beliefs of the blind automaticity of the brain.

In the centre of this grid, this thing, a tiny ant-like creature, struggles to get to the edge of the platform, but the structure itself appears to be attached to its body. And it drags the whole unwieldy structure with it, tearing at its body as it attempts to escape from itself.

Maybe all it has to do is to stop struggling? Or crawl through a hole?

Peace.

Friday 25 October 1991

PADA 46
GATHERING NECTAR

How to live creatively moment by moment?

Appreciative living is, in itself, creative. It is not so much positive thinking that is required of us, but an appreciative response to life itself, which becomes finer and finer as maturity and integration take place.

Focus and surrender. Learn to become more and more precise about what results you wish to create. Define and put colour and life and enjoyment into these intentions and visions.

Surrender the emotional attachment to them. Dwelling on perceived emotional need and past failure, sense of powerlessness and thoughts of failure slow down the creative process.

Appreciate and complete every detail of your life in the moment, and you pass. This is only possible if you live in the moment, all eyes fully open! Don't procrastinate. Appreciate, bless, complete. Move on to the next moment.

In every moment life presents itself as opportunities for shining on itself.

Practise shining wherever your attention falls. This is appreciative living, and is its own reward.

The sun shines on everything! Appreciate the movement of life behind everything.

Practise completion. Appreciation itself is an act of communion and completion.

Every day brings new seeds to nurture. At the completion of each day, gather the seeds of that day and see how your love and appreciation bathes that living potential with nourishment. Rest in appreciating the harvest at the end of each day.

See the seeds that day has planted. Appreciate what thoughts of the past have come to be dissolved.

True appreciative living is a complete practice of continual refinement, moment-by-moment. Appreciate past experiences which arise in the mind. Appreciate, bless, complete and move the gaze to the next flower. A bee gathering nectar.

PADA 47
HEARTBROKEN

It's impossible to escape from the self-transcending process of life. Living alone, or with apparent others, the all-consuming, undoing process is what is happening. This is death. Every day I become more vulnerable, more childlike, in the play, tears and laughter. Constantly heartbroken as the rawness and insensitivity is experienced, the misperceptions, the miscommunications between these seeming others, the lack of understanding of what everything is. Fortunately maybe, like a child, I don't remember from day to day, and the grief in my Heart dissipates to a certain extent. I return to a simple childlike enjoyment of the everyday events: creating a beautiful space, loving the colours, textures, shapes of the things in my room. Spending time with Barbara, learning to operate the DVD-ROM, dressing in my new clothes. When grief comes I cry, unreservedly, like a little girl, 1 am unable to control my face. I notice I give more attention to the *Grahas* at these times. These vast archetypal beings of the deep are my friends, my doorways to the wholeness of my being at these times.

1 am, Tuesday 5 December 2000

PADA 48
SUPERFLUID

What is it we are truly desiring when we think of freedom?

Freedom from those conditions that we perceive to be limiting us in any way.

Perceived lack, pain, sorrow, fear. Freedom from circumstances.

All experiences that, consciously or unconsciously, we ourselves have drawn to us.

When we resist in the slightest any aspect of our story. we are disempowering ourselves, denying our own will.

This denial actually causes conditions to persist. The mind turns to the experience of lack of freedom, slavery, imprisonment, limitation.

Freedom. What is this evocative pull?

What is it that is limitless, unbounded infinite unending? This is simply another name for our own infinite nature. Another name for love. The superfluid free state.

We are living in a prison of the past, the carapace of past circumstances, and we reflect that vibration to each other in the way we see this world, and each other. A world based on action and reaction, on mending and fixing and improving, and growth based on false premises.

The answer is here all the time, prior to all circumstances and modifications. Fresh and new in every breath. And for this to manifest in this plain, we simply look at it all as it is right now, and smile. And look with the undiscriminating eyes of a baby, and fall into the timelessness of infinity.

Gaganopamoham.

"Seek ye first the kingdom of heaven and all these things shall be added to you."

True freedom lies in realising your already pre-existing freedom. Making this REAL. Surrendering to EMBODYING that living presence. Superfluid.

You become what you put your attention on. This is **law**.

PADA 49
FOOTPRINTS

It is not so much healing the mind that is required, as correcting the residual distorted mental structures which are the occasion of erroneous perception of the world. *Pragya Paradh*. These false structures are actually embodied, creating the archaeological body.

The way an individual perceives and experiences the world is encoded in the instrument. The mental, emotional and physical structure, the body, which is, of course, also Mind! We identify true crystalline flow, which is inherent and arises spontaneously from Being to reinforce this true expression. We cease to energise the archaeology, and facilitate its dissolution and integration.

A structure which is truly alive is a dynamic flow, a pattern of living energy with rhythms and tides, ebb and flow, like the ocean. The repeated patterns on the beach merely show where the movement of the ocean has been. Consider a man walking on the beach. Feet moving one in front of the other. The footprints are already dead. They simply show where he has been…

PADA 50
THE ONLY FOCUS

Wherever we look there is only one thing to see! What are we looking at? What is everything?

We are not here for ourselves. For what we **think** we are. For what we **seem** to have been. For our old structure. We are not here to fill what we experience as yearning emptiness.

We are here appearing spontaneously, as spaces for love, bliss, nectar to flow through. And this doesn't even begin to say it properly! We are here **only** for this. To remember. To join up the dots, to know everything for what it actually is, so it is known as only Reality.

To integrate everything into our experience, and know that this world of form is simply a kaleidoscope of love, a magnificent magic show to be enjoyed by the silent witness. It is not a question of healing the body, physical or emotional or mental.

Though we can simply do what seems to be intelligent for our wellbeing. We are here to be the silence, knowing and enjoying itself. Return to the experience of the original matrix is then possible, but this is not the primary focus.

Love, silence, stillness are the real focus, and then everything automatically is experienced for what it is. We get to enjoy it all. The whole of the movie.

When the whole is embraced without exception, judgement fades, dissolves, and we experience only the Heart.

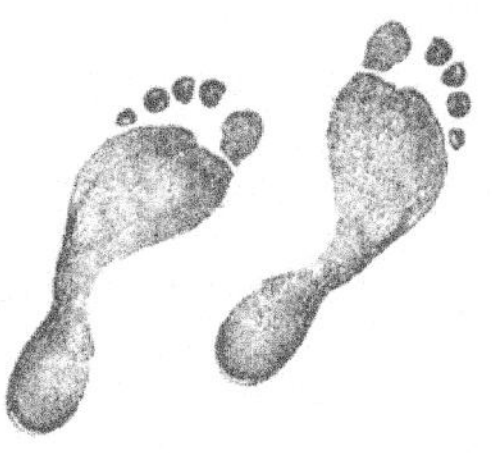

PADA 51
WHAT ARE YOU LOOKING AT?

Appreciating this world without exception is to be an alchemist.

To many, the world appears to be under a spell. The world at a certain frequency appears to be conditioned to see itself through the eyes of separative personality.

What it sees are the shards of the Ice Queen's mirror, and so believes what it sees and experiences. What it sees is little, powerless, contracted, out of focus, untrue. What it then sees **with**, also appears as little, powerless, contracted, out of focus, untrue. The instrument of perception is modified and becomes unclear. It believes its treasure is broken, and needs to be mended.

I am here to see this world for what it is, as living treasure, and to see with what it is, a living Heart.

I am here to see through the spell, to open the eyes of the Heart, to see with the eyes of love, to love it all, every detail, into becoming Real. As I see the treasure, so shall is.

What do you want to be here for?

I choose to see what is Real. And so it is. I love this world of seeming dross as treasure, and so it is. The Heart is broken over and over again, as the Ice

Queen's mirror reflects partial vision. The Heart is a phoenix, always rising from the debris of the years. And the Heart can never accept what the mote in the eye appears to show.

I am here to love it all into wholeness. When the mirror seems to shatter I am here to shine on it, to love it all into wholeness. It is a simple choice of moment-by-moment perception. To restore what seems broken or untrue with the glance of a Christed one!

I am here to 'heal' the broken-hearted by seeing them as whole. To speak the good news of life. Nothing more.

The filters of perception and judgement will prevent you from seeing the world in its true colours, make it appear broken. True perception reveals incredible flowering. We do this to each other all the time, consciously and unconsciously, by not seeing true identity. A plant can flourish or wither according to how it is regarded. A water crystal can be beautiful or distorted, depending on the intention behind the focus directed at it. The beauty is innate, and reveals itself to those who choose to see.

We are all here for this. We are all here to lift the spell. To be alive in Treasure Eyeland. To live as the Heart, blessing all beings, all things. Who will commit to it?

Commitment changes the way nature responds, changes the face of the world, brings all kinds of helping circumstances that would otherwise not have happened.

One of the greatest gifts we have is our ability to choose where to place our attention, and define our intention. We have the power of life and death. Will you bless or curse? Will you look with the eye of Medusa, or that of a little child? Will you look into the mirror with appreciation, or will you pick at the spots on the silvering of the mirror, and watch the beauty dissolve?

Whatever you see that is not appreciated is simply unappreciated structure – which can harden into negative structure if not seen for what it actually is. Love, tenderness, since that is all there is.

I am committed to love this world of shadows into being Treasure Eyeland. It only takes one in any situation.

Who will commit to perceiving this Treasure with the eyes of the Heart?

Will you side with what is Real, or what is unreal?

PADA 52
MONEYFRUIT!

There's money in my cupboards
Overflowing on the shelves
And moneyjars for visitors
Please come and help yourselves!

And money in my garden
Wild and strong like weeds
Filling all the flowerbeds
Where I planted moneyseeds

Money blossoms bursting
With pollen for the bees
Promising abundant harvest
Wealth from my moneytrees

Moneyfruit is dropping
Windfalls from the trees
Bounty to be gathered
As far as you can see!

Money clouds overhead
Moneyweather clear to see
Now moneydrops are raining
Silver puddles for you and me!

Moneystars are shining
Treasure in the night
Pocketfuls of golden moneydust
To do with whatever you like!

My Christmas gifts are ready
They're all homemade this year
From new varieties of moneyfruit
You'll be very pleased to hear!

Bearer bonds and cheque accounts
I grew them fresh and clean
With love and imagination
And wrapped them in gold and green!

Money floating everywhere
A magic shining sea
Abundant boundless oceans
Of energy for free!

Kishori Jeanette McKenzie, November 2004

PADA 53
THAT MYSTERIOUS SECRET

There is a mysterious secret to living this life. The understanding of the way things truly are, and how life flows. Mysterious, that is, only to the Mind, of hard edges and definition into objects and sequential events, and their surface relationship to each other. Mind, which defines and separates everything into objective reality.

To that silent spaciousness, that we can call Quantum Heart, source of our imagination and point of arising of all temporary conditions, nothing is mysterious, all is intrinsically interconnected and enfolded into itself.

Most of humanity puts its attention on the surface objective world and identifies with that, and that state of mind which takes a 'thing' to be what mind says it is, and maintains it in the peripheral perception of the way things are.

Let your perception and attention and curiosity about the way things are fall for a moment into the Quantum Reality of the Heart source, and be curious to recognise the non-relational state, and everything changes like night into day. Solid objects come to life and become superfluid. Particles become waves flowing into each other. Cinderella's fairy godmother appears and the world becomes a magical place where miracles are natural events, and opportunities flower on every piece of waste land.

Since childhood I have looked to bring that land of the Heart that I know so well into tangible form in a living community of the Heart, where all, everyone and everything, is satisfied in a magical way, where we slip through the cracks of this sharply-defined world.

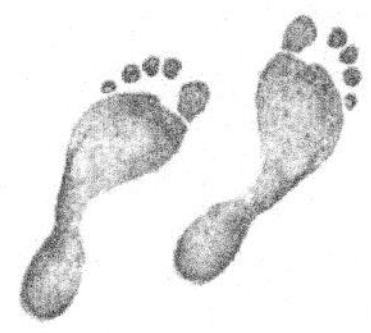

PADA 54
WATER POURED OUT

I am emptying myself to infinity.

When completion comes, in every breath, I revert to a state of absolute stillness, non-existence in form, annihilation, giving myself fully, to infinity, to all my selves who come to drink. With thoughtless simplicity, childlike, I resist nothing, giving all. Vulnerable like water poured out, filling the place where I happen to be. Becoming the desire of all. Surrendered into silence.

I flow into form, fragmenting through the prism mind, shattering into a myriad jewelled moments. I see and embrace it all passionately, move to unite with myself - breathing, absorbing, loving, consuming, sucking it all into myself.

A constant systole and diastole. An endless lovemaking. An eternal *puja* to myself. My Heart beating it all. Loving every breath. Emptying and filling, expanding and contracting. The breath of existence. The rhythm of simplicity. Each day, each breath, each moment – a jewelled pulsation, a shimmering starburst, a sparkling drop on a spider's web of perfection.

All enfolded to infinity in this eternal Now. Complete in every heartbeat. Creating and drowning anew in every breath, in each delicious, fractaline impulse of the lingam. All this my own form. All my own bliss.

Shakti consumed in the soft breath of Shiva.

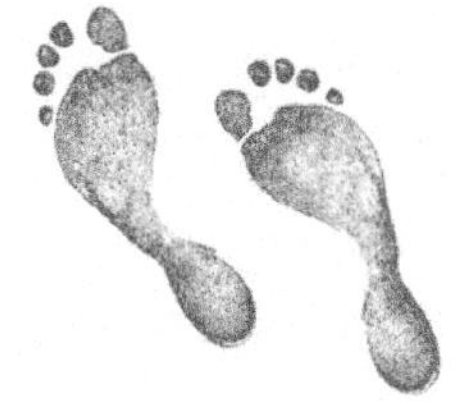

PADA 55
FLIGHT OF THE ARROW

Any apparently self-contained ecological system may seek to exert pressure or control on what it perceives to be external to itself, in a misguided attempt to balance the pressure it experiences, which is, in fact, arising from within what it perceives to be itself.

This externally-projected force, or attempt to control, will be in direct proportion to the amount of pressure it experiences as arising from within, all the while believing that which is seemingly external to itself to be the source of the experienced pressure.

All desire, however, is for legitimate expression and eventually must be satisfied. There is ultimately only one mind. All is arising within **mind**. The impulse behind the desire must lead to flow, or it stagnates.

A fear-based system is a house built on sand. Maya. The Matrix. A fear-based system will attempt to control its environment, which it mirrors to itself by its erroneous perception of the actions of 'others., Domination, denial, manipulation, suppression, a myriad different ways. Caught in the belief in ownership of its world. What a burden! Responsibility for the chaotic universe!

Each system is an entire universe creating its own dream, and from the perspective of the apparent individual there can be no agreement with 'another' system. Each one, at the relative level, is entirely alone, entirely responsible for their story, and the response. Each one caught in their own bubble, their own frame of reference.

Relative perception does not exist for the Absolute, which always sweetly includes all lenses in the holographic eye as valid, of equal value, 'Equi-va-lent' (pronounced equi-**vay**-lent). Only through the Heart do we know each other, touch each other. Only through the Heart can we truly enjoy and delight in each other's story.

If I get a 'chill' this is an event entirely in my dream.

And all dreams can be interpreted to reveal the underlying belief system, in the deeper psyche, the unconscious, archetypal realities. The apparent events in our life arise from our beliefs and programmes.

It's not quite like that. Being simply radiates. Individual possessive mind distorts. Layers of impacted mind produce thicker or thinner veils, superimpositions on what has no need of anything. Modifications of Reality. But all this is only experientially.

In truth nothing is touched, nothing is modified. All remains always eternally at home in the Heart. We can allow our story to be a dance suffused with the sun shining from the still point of our knowing, or we can be caught like a leaf in the wind of our deceiving mind.

In Reality though, every apparently separate universe is a bud, a blossom on the tree of life. Every one of us is a child universe, free to be, to flower as we choose. But only when we know what we truly are, that we are not our own, is this possible.

Only then is the power of the Heart truly available to us. Only then can the sap from the root flow to the non-separate bud, the baby world, the newness. It can only come from the Source, the tree of life.

I am the flight of the arrow.

Reflections, 1999

PADA 56
WEAVER BIRD

Like a weaver bird I built the nest of this old body
Hoarding treasure piece by piece
In winding alchemical byways
Tubes and tunnels and blind alleys
A home of undigested memories and echoing
bones

Now I am bursting out, throwing it all away
Scattering my crust of fool's gold to the winds
Dancing wild and free
An endless thread of streaming song
Spiralling naked in the sun

Kishori Devi, 16 May 2006

PADA 57
LIVING ALCHEMY

I am an alchemist conducting research into the nature and dynamics of consciousness, the physics of relationship of objects. In truth there is only subject. When all is experienced as subject, this is the state beyond relationship.

Life is a process of alchemy. The apparent movement of life is energised by the unconscious attraction of opposite contents, followed by the elimination or dissolution of this energy when merging, neutralisation, assimilation, or digestion, has been completed.

The experience of desire for an apparent object or other is a sign of this magnetic attraction, a positive pull towards integration. The experience of repulsion is also an indication of a powerful negative unconscious magnetic force.

Life is a continual integration process, then further apparent disintegration which looks and feels chaotic, followed by elimination of the completed projects, and further redefinition, a continual refining process. The completed projects are no longer energised, and so seem to have simply been erased.

Eventually, by witnessing, everything becomes a conscious non-egoic, choiceful play rather than a magnetic automatic attraction of unconscious opposites to each other in order to produce a new synthesis. Only those projects which are energised in consciousness are available to be experienced.

This, then, is the question. When the energy of unconscious attraction is no longer the driving force, when the process of polarising and merging is no longer the fuel for life and some kind of equilibrium is reached, then what next? This is the place beyond separation, the state of conscious awakened union, home. Buddhi, the light at the doorway, is constantly witnessing, enjoying, understanding this process of digestion.

The structure of Jeanette as a set of surface bodies, is in a constant state of metastable equilibrium, pulling towards stable equilibrium. Constantly destabilising to reach a finer and finer integration. She appears to the observer to move between perceiving with the precision of a scientist and the intense clarity of a Zen master, or drowning in the chaos of irrationality, dysfunction and disintegration! In fact she does not move. She witnesses the alchemical process, the union of opposites!

What next?!

PADA 58
DUTY OR DELIGHT

It is never a question of what do I **have** to do.

It is simply a question of how you will express your love.

What will you do for love?

What is your true desire? Your Divine Desire?

How much will your actions give space for and express your love for that liquid living fire? How will you feed that passion? With the blood from your own breast. As the pelican feeds its young. Wounding its own heart to feed its newborn. Pie Pelicanis.

How much life story will you keep to feed this illusory idea, the story of 'yourself'? Or will you choose to give everything to this divine desire… for this alone?

Can you learn to listen and smell and taste, and wait upon the movement of the flow of the inner river with the attentiveness of a mother for the subtleties of the breath of her newborn as he sighs in his sleep?

Can you allow the flame of your love to be fanned to such a conflagration that Shiva himself is awakened by the heat of the *tapasya* to fall completely into the fire of love? Consumed by and overflowing with the simplicity of this Passionate Presence.

And the stones dance and the mountains bow in response.

That beautiful Hymn I used to sing as a child comes to mind:

"Teach me my God and King,
In all things Thee to see,
That what I do in everything,
To do it as for Thee."

To allow Implicate Order and Abundance to be all there is, knowing, experience, passion and bliss.

We are creating **love** in form. Whatever it may look like to Mind. The liquid fire flows and moves from its own phoenix-like Source.

I breathe in and I inhale Shiva's breath. I breathe out and he inhales the breath of this body. Together we perform the tantric *Hieros Gamos*. The Sacred Dance. He and she and she and me. Together we create union – Alchemy - intoxication. He is the space and she is the dancing liquid fire. Together we are one. There is only one priority: To catch fire with this Passion. *"They will come from everywhere to watch you burn."*

30 January 2008

PADA 59
IMAGINATION

"*Imagination is more important than knowledge. For knowledge is limited, whereas imagination embraces the entire world, stimulating progress, giving birth to evolution.*"- Einstein

What is this distortion, this acid overlay, this chip of ice in the eye that gives rise to the experience of alienation, fragmentation, loss, suffering, abandonment, abuse, terrorism, crime, despair? This film of slime covering the vast pulsating living emptiness?

This destruction and distorted perception which makes our world's beautiful children into victims of abuse, criminals, thieves, terrorists? Creating monstrous refugees out of innocence and beauty, castrating this radiant power, simplicity, vision, the impulse to sing and dance and create.

Daridrya dukha dahanaya, namah shivaya!
Remove poverty and the dearth of wealth!

We are to create from the Source of innocence, not from reaction, blindness and automaticity.

Each is able to empower themselves. Each can dream and bring forth from their treasure, and respond to that blissful flowing spontaneous Keyala. Each can remind the world's children, both our inner children and the outer children of the streets, to dare to **dream**… and to dream big.

26 June 2010

PADA 60
STEER INTO THE SKID!

The bottom line is this. Steer into the Skid! Let go of resistance! Just being in whatever seems to be happening will lead automatically into freedom. Stop seeking anything with insistence.

Searching for anything more than the simplicity of what is unfolding in the moment triggers suffering. An emotional seeking for more is a hunger which cannot be filled. It already is what it is, already fullness itself. Already happiness.

Therefore seeking is not the key if it is seen as offering an answer to a perceived problem. Though it can provide some understanding, and inviting attention to rest in what is Real, which is the solution to all perceived lack or difficulty. Searching to be free of pain or uncomfortable emotions, or dysfunctional behaviour, or an 'improved spiritual state', keeps one in the experience of separation.

Life is simply living itself. One whose attention is on the Real becomes the Real. Being with one whose attention is on the Real is a catalyst for that to become the case in others. It is simply consciousness opening to itself.

Authentic Living is the ability to be in the moment, continually returning to rest in every breath, holding onto nothing, not building castles in the air. Resting in the nothing. The mind sees something unfolding from Being, and will run after it to get more of it. The knack of authentic living is to observe and let it be.

The bottom line is that of course nothing needs to be different. However, if within the story we simply become curious about the structure in which we seem to exist, and we choose to explore it, interesting effects seem to take place. Attention, love, is a most amazing flow! A fulcrum with which to move the world!

This exploration or inquiry can begin at any point, by looking at our life story, patterns, lineage, relationships, exploring through bodywork. Observation in itself is alchemy. As we cease believing in the separateness of the world around us and we turn our attention back to the source of our existence, and the origin of the particular viewpoint of consciousness as this apparently individual point of focus, an experience of integration takes place.

It is eventually realised that there is no 'we'. No 'I'. There is simply this diffuse awareness. This is the difference between Reality and experience. No-thing and the experience of the dance.

Awareness traces itself back through the Pandora's box doorway into Reality.

Ramana spoke of following the I thought to its source in the Heart. When consciousness begins to put attention on this point of arising, witnessing the cosmic display, life begins to appear as it truly is, a kaleidoscopic magic show, for entertainment of the Self.

The illusory sense of personal limited existence falls away, and undigested experience begins to be consumed and transformed in what can be likened to an alchemical process, turning life into an experience of pleasurable freedom and play.

We know that observation of a situation will alter it entirely. The observer is not separate from what he or she observes. It is simply consciousness observing its own play, *"a long thin umbilical periscope, backbending, craning its neck to see, self cognising self"*, from one of my poems.

PADA 61
TWO WORLDS

Two worlds – seemingly – and only one is true. Shall I look at the surface, or live from the deep?

In December 2001 I am visiting Tapovarista Asramam in northern Kerala, sitting on the floor in front of the Master, Sri Tathata. He is the beautiful gentle Master of this Indian ashram, only frequented by very few westerners. There too are a couple of Maitri, his long-standing disciples. It is very hot, as usual, and I am dressed in a South Indian light muslin sari. I had supposed the meeting would be *darshan*, but it turns into an interview. One of the senior Maitri, who was called Father, is translating since Sri Tathata preferred not to speak in English unless necessary.

First I am told I can give an account of myself to the Master. I sit there and look at him, and just laughter comes. I spread my hands in a gesture of impossibility, and more laughter comes, and he is laughing too. It seems completely impossible to begin to say anything about who is sitting here. Eventually I say something about having let everything go some years earlier. Then Father asks me, "What is your spiritual practice?" I can't think of anything I am practising any more! I decide to say

I am just living, not practising anything in particular. I think about saying nothing, or my practice is just looking at things and enjoying them, but the truth is that I hadn't thought about such things as spiritual practice for a long time. Instead, the latest communication I seem to have received on the subject of what I am doing here comes to mind. I decide to tell him the following story:

"I am walking along a little country road, which borders the beautiful artificial lake in the village of Neyyerdam, reflecting on my life, some months earlier in the year, watching a villager tenderly washing his buffalo in the morning sun.

They seem to be shining, and I am completely enjoying the devotion of man and animal. As I watch the play of life and devotion between the two, wondering what my next step in life is to be, the inner voice seems to say, "I have digested your life, your house, your friends, your career, and now I am digesting this body!"

I guess this information will probably be appropriate, and I offer it to Sri Tathata. He laughs, obviously amused. Father, translating, says the Master very much likes what I had said. Anyway, they don't ask me any more about my practice. I am simply playing India, as always, following my 'cabbage white butterfly', my spontaneous Keyala, the Leela, story or loveplay, of my Heart.

A few days later I am leaving the Ashram, and go to say goodbye. I stand there, anticipating possibly more mantra, or a recommended *Sadhana.* Sri Tathata looks deeply into my eyes and says, "For you, no *Sadhana* is necessary". I namaste and I walk away, a huge sense of relief in my heart, since I really don't want any more practice. I haven't seen any difference between so-called 'spiritual' and so-called 'material' for a long time.

25 December 2001

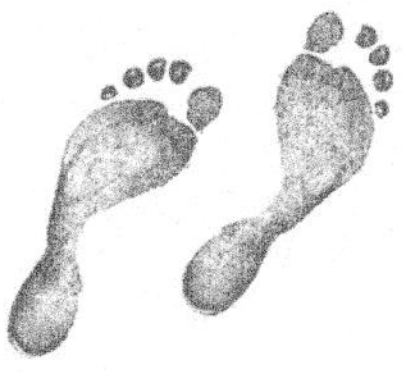

PADA 62
GAZING FROM EMPTINESS

The Magic of Conscious Relating

How we engage with the Shadow, the energy of the ungrown, the unevolved, the fearful, the denied, is a key to all so-called problems, individual or collective. The habitual reflex of fight or flight, freeze or resist, attack or defend, criticise or judge, does not work.

In this process of Communicating from the Heart, we can experience how simple it is to gaze and connect from Emptiness, with the eyes of a baby, giving the kiss of Beauty to the Beast.

Truth, like beauty, or blindness, is always in the eye of the beholder.

To see and be simply that Truth, whatever it may look like, is a choice to be made. A little, almost imperceptible, shift in perception into the silent 'Now' in the Heart, can transform everything in the moment, melting walls and miraculously changing outcomes.

When the Eye of the Heart sees beyond the surface of the personality, there is a concentration like a laser beam, a burning of the fossil fuel of old programming, and the walls of the past begin to dissolve.

It is not difficult to see in this way. It is our natural state. To see with the eye of a child. It takes only a little willingness and a little courage to begin.

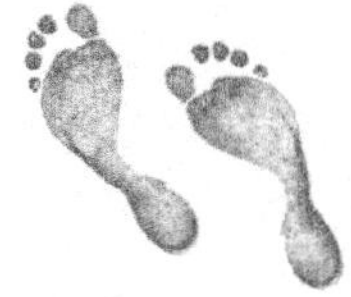

PADA 63
THE WAY HOME

This world of holographic images of light and sound when experienced in this dimension, as an apparently closed system, can appear to swing crazily from one extreme to another, as a pendulum, in order to fulfil the impulse towards balance, equilibrium. So operates the seeming law of cause and effect in this plane. In fact, all this is a spontaneous display of light and sound, flowing with immediacy, in the moment, as the sound current from what we can call the original Word. When it is left to Be as it arises, it is simply this flow of Living Presence, appearing in these crystalline forms in this dimension, ever changing, ever new, ever wondrous. Being spontaneously delighting in its own expression.

When separative mind puts pressure on any part of this display with a view to strategically modifying it, to suit the desire or perception of a fragmented indrawing consciousness, this distorts the whole experience. It fixes attention in this plane, disturbing the infinitely fine balance of the living current. To live easily in this dimension you need to walk softly as a little kitten, allowing things to be as they are, enjoying it all, participating gently and tenderly.

Living in the moment, knowing this truth, and the polarising effect of distortion comes to rest, and true expression spontaneously reverts to the world of appearances. The magic show displays once again in its true living colours!

Forcefully controlling the swing of a pendulum does not make it come to rest. Denying and controlling a powerful, experienced need cannot empty the energy, the tension, locked in it. Better to allow it to gracefully die, to slow and complete the momentum of its own accord by bringing attention to the true flow of real life. Attending to the Real, the momentum of the unreal disappears from lack of energy. The experience of Truth spontaneously returns, because Truth is all that is left.

We cease to repress what we have judged unacceptable in this dimension, and energy of what we call shadow is allowed to emerge and integrate. Light and shade are both aspects of the Real, as seen in this dimension through the filters, which operate in order to allow this dimension to be experienced. Preferring and rejecting one pole of matter over the other will trap your consciousness in this material plain. Wholeness is truth here, not so-called goodness. This is a mental judgement coming from the mechanical surface instrument, which we call the mental body. The mental body does not truly think. Its function is to simply reflect what is already known. Every thing, every idea, every invention already exists in this moment in the eternal mind, simply flowing itself into form!

To return to true embodiment, integration of the shadow must be allowed. And this is a delicate matter, as so much repressed energy has accumulated in the region of darkness that it has to be addressed with delicacy. It is not a question of simply opening Pandora's Box and allowing the forces of terrorism and abuse to be unleashed. Each apparently individual fragment of the Infinite Mind, each cell of the infinite consciousness, is to examine gently, and allow itself to consider and integrate the repressed disallowed experiences, judgements of its story, its portion of the collective darkness of this plain, allowing this energy to be digested.

This material dimension - matter, mother, feminine - is also the negative pole of consciousness, and the positive pole, which we could call masculine, if this did not evoke all sorts of judgements about male and female in this plane. It is compelled by the law of wholeness (love), to reach out to itself, to embrace itself in form. It is all a dance! This is where the stories originate of the spaceships waiting for the Earth to come to its senses. And Shakti dancing in frenzy on the corpse of Shiva. They are archetypal stories attempting to explain the alchemical movements of consciousness, 'longing' to know itself awake in form.

Acceptance of all, gentle, tender allowing of the integration of the shadow, is the way to see Reality, is the only way Home. The individual eye is a lens, one facet of the full spectrum diamond eye of consciousness, seeing all, including all. With the shutter closed in contraction (fear, self-interest), all you can see is the dust on the inside of the lens, or total darkness. Allowing all that is unconscious to rise, to be seen and known and come to neutral, is the desire of the Heart to come to rest.

Reality-love is impersonal, like the shining of the sun, until it becomes the play of the differentiated little sunbeam.

Rua Conselheiro Joaquim Machado, Lagos,
6 October 2002

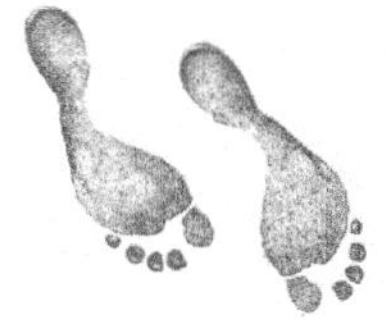

PADA 64
THE COMING OF THE DARK ONES

A story exploring Rahu as the Beloved (part of a series)

I am in the garden behind my castle. Some weeks have gone by since I first came to Sanctuary, as it is a little later in the year, and warmer. It is late morning and I have the thought that I would like to build the little white house with the central courtyard that I saw when I was initially approaching the building that turned into the castle.

So, I ask the drawer of water from the well, whose name he tells me is Jason, to organise a building team. He finds some of the castle retainers and they are all very happy to help with my new project.

We begin to mark out a space near the bottom of the garden on one of the green lawns. The house is built of smooth white stone with a shiny surface like marble. It is built quite quickly, an arched door for an entrance. It looks rather Spanish, with rooms in a square all opening onto the central courtyard, and a splashing fountain in the middle. There are piles of white stones and blue glazed pots of flowers, full white daisies and bright pink geraniums with love-in-a-mist, and deep blue lobelia trailing from the pots. Purple bougainvillea climbs up one white wall between the tall French windows, which are open, soft muslin curtains shifting slightly in the faint breeze.

Inside there is a light, clean, contemporary decor, pale wooden floors, white walls, green plants, low tables with bowls of scented jasmine. There are fantastic contemporary bathrooms with the latest state-of-the-art white furniture. The magnificent contemporary kitchen is also white, with washed pale turquoise wooden doors, and touches of silver everywhere. All appliances are concealed.

There is an oval glass table in one corner with a silver bowl of ripe wild strawberries, a bottle of champagne cooling in ice, and silver goblets.

I furnish one beautiful room with full length mirrors, low lights, soft floor cushions, sofas and mattresses in creams and whites, peaches and apricots. It is completely luscious.

As the shadows lengthen and the evening draws in, the workmen begin to pack up and say goodnight. We decide to furnish the rest of the house tomorrow. They leave me relaxing in the courtyard, eating the strawberries and contemplating Sanctuary life.

So far I seem to have a castle, hardly explored, and a team of faithful diligent retainers, a wellman called Jason, an old nurse called Demelza, an

Arabian palace with a retinue of beautiful women, a loving dresser called Sundari, spacious well-kept gardens, a forest full of paradise and wild animals, a bear sanctuary, an eagle, and a lucky white dragon who smiles (like in *The NeverEnding Story*). I have met an elven magician and The Choice Master, and an Extraordinary Heart Being who dissolves dysfunction. I seem to have acquired the power to ask trees to give me fruit, and to merge with eagles and bears, and space and stars. And now I have built a contemporary hacienda-style home.

I am prepared to continue enjoying this new home. I have even planned a tantric meditation evening in my new space, and have invited a few chosen guests to come later to play, when suddenly my attention is drawn to activity over to the left, back nearer to the trees, to the north of the shiny new white hacienda.

Dark shadows are emerging from the forest. I am drawn to leave my elegant, pristine new house and investigate. There is a powerful energy attracting me to them, like the compelling feeling of love for the wild animals at the beginning of Sanctuary.

The shadows continue to come, and are carrying various artefacts with them.

"Who are you?" I ask. "And what do you want?"

"We are your Dark Friends, the dark magicians from deep in the forest, and beyond, my Lady. We are here to serve you in your deepest desires, your darkest and most secret wounds, for your emerging wholeness."

I feel myself begin to sob uncontrollably.

"We are the lovers of the trees. The nameless ones. We see in the night, and we are here because you have loved us, and befriended us, and called us with your longing. You have poured life into us over many years. The moment for us to meet has arrived. It is time to build you a home to match your energy, a shape for your original blueprint." They are faceless, dark shapes, dressed in shadowy black cloaks.

They begin to mark out a smallish square plot near the trees at the edge of the forest, placing four stones that they have brought with them, one at each corner of the plot. They chant, "Earth, Air, Fire, Water... And Space in the middle of the house where She must sit."

I stand a few yards away from the north east corner of the plot, and watch mesmerised. I am fascinated, and deeply moved. The Dark Ones are reminiscent of something from Lord of the Rings, or an Elizabeth Goudge tale, from when I was a child.

Some of the faceless ones now start to dig a square pit in front of the house. They fill it with stones and light a fire. I wonder... are they going to perform a *homa*? But that happens in India, and here it is the west.

A very tall Dark One comes to stand at my right side as I watch the activity. Night has come and it is now quite dark, but for the flickering flames from the fire pit. There is no moon, and the stars are hardly visible.

The feeling as he stands beside me is indescribable. He is focused, powerful and magnetic. He emanates a completely solid presence. I am feeling extremely vulnerable, remembering the struggle I had to get here, and the deep wounds the Dark Ones spoke of. An exquisite tenderness flows from him and I dissolve into deep sobs. I realise that he SEES me... to the core. He appears to KNOW me… and also himself. I am aware that they have all come to answer an unconscious ache, to fill a chasm in the earth and this aspect of the lineage I inherited, I have dreamt of being filled. The kind of endless longing, screaming from the guts and the throat of the horse in Picasso's *Guernica*.

He barely touches my arm. "Look... they are preparing your land, making the foundation stable."

"Other Dark Ones are now clearing the ground under the house they are to build, making the base of the dream sustainable."

The Dark Ones create a great space in the earth and fill it with rods of light and copper and crystals, an intricate network far, far into the centre of the earth and beyond. As we watch they use lasers to clear backwards and forwards in time, till past and future meet in a loop, and upwards in space and outwards in a magical, restorative, protective shimmering blue-white shield. We walk over to feel the energy. It feels full, soft, infinitely springy, a supporting cloud. There is nowhere to fall to!

Now more of the Dark Ones are bringing cedar trees with which they quickly build the house, the foundations magically sinking deep into the earth. They put green branches on the roof and a smooth wooden floor, a simple wooden door with a latch to lift to enter, and a circular copper disk with an intricate design above the door.

My new friend takes my arm, and we walk over to the firepit and stand gazing down at the white-hot, incandescent stones, feeling the intensity of the rising heat haze. I am beginning to feel as if I have known him for a very long time.

"Who are you?" I wonder.

He laughs. "We have had this conversation already, once upon a time..."

"Have we met before?"

"Not in this form, but you have always known me."

"Is there a name I can call you?"

"I have many names. Here I am Cor Lucis, but you can call me Luceo if you prefer." As I look at him, streams of energy like ripples of light flow from the centre of his forehead. He appears completely solid, like obsidian. Now in the centre of his chest there is a disk of coloured light, spinning.

"Come." I sense him hold out what must be a hand. "We can walk through the fire now.
Are you ready?"

I realise the fire is not a *homa,* but a ritual cleansing for me.

"Yes, I am ready."

Strangely I feel no fear. He takes my hand, and I step out with him, into the fire. We don't so much walk as glide though the fire, over the stones.

My robe disintegrates in the heat but I am not burnt. I am shining. I am naked, but also clothed in luminous, shimmering waves of colour, like the rotating disk in his Heart. He is now a kind of indeterminate dark radiance.

We quietly reach the other side of the firepit, and enter the cedar house for the first time. I am still clothed in my multicoloured energy robe, and he in his dark radiance.

The scent of cedar wood is delicious. The house is just one simple room inside. The door faces east towards the sea, and the rising sun, as do all my dwellings in this place. In the corner to the left as we enter there is a large comfortable bed with a soft fleecy white cover made out of something like sheep's wool, and on the smooth wooden floor there is a woven rug in intricate ancient patterns of red and orange. Opposite the door is a wood-burning stove, doors open to the fire inside. A magical spring of water in the south-west corner, a comfortable sofa, and a wooden table with fruit and a flask of wine are to the north side of the room.

"The rest of the furnishing you can create later, or we can do this together if it pleases you."

“Now rest...” He leads me to the bed, and I lie down on the white softness.

“I can leave you here alone, or I can sit by the fire while you sleep, or I can lie quietly here beside you while you sleep. You choose.”

23 March 2008

PADA 65
DRAWN TOGETHER

We are drawn together apparently by individual choice, becoming ever more open to exploring the Mystery of Life. And we all know that there are deep, powerful currents to which we have already opened our Hearts, which we fell in love with, and which carry us inevitably to experience our Heart's desire.

At this point in the birthing of the New Earth, so much turbulence is being experienced everywhere, in Nature, in society, in our individual lives. We are in transition from a 3D world in object referral, to one of living from the non-dual state, in reference only to our Being, in self-referral.

Being part of a community choosing this state of wholeness facilitates our choice and supports the focus we must hold to withdraw attention from the way society currently thinks and behaves and emotes. We aim to anchor in a state of appreciation for this gift of ever unfolding Life, and extend this coherence to each other and all beings.

Our bottom line is that Life, Reality, is communicating with us, who are the expression of Life, unceasingly. This is the case 24/7! The Living Mystery is in communion with itself, without separation. Whatever our experience may be right now this is the Truth.

The Rahu material and the practice of welcoming the shadow, the *atithi,* is a recognition of this.

We are Infinite Imagination and we have great gifts, willingness, desire, courage and capacity to **feel**. Our intuition is becoming ever more valuable. Each Heart makes its own choice, of course, but the power of **together** is vast, reflecting the simplicity of love and attention, to each other!

PADA 66
DIGESTING LIFE

We can look at the way we eat food, digest and eliminate in the body as an out-picturing of the way we consume life.

Life was designed to be enjoyed freely and spontaneously for the simple enjoyment of **being**. An experience comes. We live it, enjoy it, digest it, integrate the experience, feel satisfied, and let it go.

Except we don't! Don't always let it go, that is! Fear, conditioning, other negative contracted attitudes, tension, stress, anxiety, regret, guilt, anger, prevent us from living fully in the moment. So, we hold our breath…

Then what happens?

We don't fully live the experience. We decide to sort it out later. Tense up. Bury our head. Put it on hold.

The Result?

Stagnation, procrastination, paralysis, rage, misery, lack, loss, absence, pressure in the system, loneliness, abandonment, contraction, pain. On many levels!

All this is: energetic and emotional constipation!

When we resolve to clean up our life and really go for it,your inner 'file manager' starts to release old stuff, old programmes, old files. And our conscious mind says 'Oh no! That is **not** what I intended to happen'. And starts to worry. But it is no more than doing a physical detox. Your body will naturally start to release. You may sweat more, you may have extra bowel movements; you might get more mucous as it eliminates, even a sore throat or flu-like symptoms. And **nothing** is wrong. It is simply taking the opportunity to discard what it doesn't need.

When you begin to take clear focused steps towards creating a massive grounded change in your life, begin to say, "Well yes, actually I would prefer to thaw out and be fully **alive**. I would like to be radiantly happy. And yes, actually it might look like being in a new more coherent relationship. Hmmm, I can see I would enjoy being friends with money, and receiving an annual income in excess of, say, £100,000 or £1,000,000. Or being more creative, and more…" My Being does deserve to experience abundant vitality and health in this body, a great career, and all those other experiences which express the unbounded, abundant flow of Truth.

So, what are **you** going to offer your Beloved Being?

What is more intelligent and fun to put most of your excited attention on, and grow into?

A quick trip to the emotional loo, so to speak? No big deal! It happens! And it's gone! You can practise emotional and energetic hygiene by regularly releasing old stuff that really wants to go! Recycling the blocked energy.

Or what about consciously creating a beautiful, delicious, colourful, abundant banquet of life, with variety and goodness and fun and pleasure and celebration, for your Inner Beloved and **you** to enjoy together?

It's a no-brainer! Begin to design your life deliberately, short, medium and long term. Day-by-day be curious to experience and share the increasing blessings, gifts and changes, as the seeds of your true desire grow.

Choose, as well, to give space to let the old release, be recycled, and composted! And see and share what happens as you recognise and acknowledge both processes.

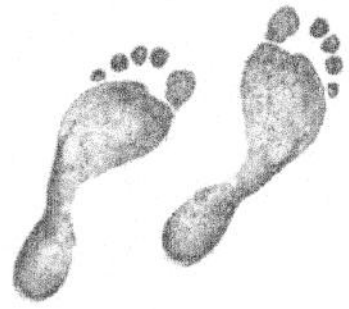

PADA 67
INNER BELOVED

When you live in union with yourself and allow that inner authentic love affair with your Self to come alive, you become Real. You awaken to the realisation that all outer experience in this world, without exception, is a reflection, an expression of your own essential nature. You can lose nothing, except by your choice. You can make those choices more and more consciously, and realise that any circumstances in life that you have not yet mastered are not set in stone. We are children, growing, expanding into unlimited Mastery.

This knowledge in itself can bring great freedom, relaxation, joy and intense relief. And creates the desire to know the wonder that we actually are, and can become, in form, more and more fully. There is always more to discover and to master and to surrender to allowing. Our inner treasure is really unlimited... and flows into form… so it becomes something tangible and visible. Love flows into something we can touch and taste… in matter.

Your Being, your Inner Beloved, in all forms, becomes ever more attractive. Irresistible! When you begin to allow yourself to fall in love with Who and What you actually are, your current limited identity is lost. This is the experience of Rumi and the mystics. Together we are engaged in this mysterious process of awakening to that treasure. Which is experienced wonderfully in a unique, intensely personal way. Union. The *Hieros Gamos*. Extraordinary, yet mysteriously practical and nourishing in a personal way.

Let's see what happens next! Step by step. Keep sharing what you experience and what seems to happen. This magnifies the potential. I am curious to see what we will create! We are a culture of the Real! Of authenticity, of freedom from the illusion of limitation! Never been done in this way before!

And we have only just begun...

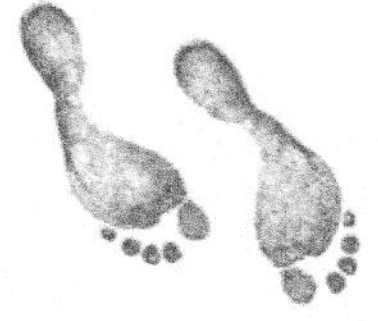

PADA 68
BECOMING ONE

What you are is One, single, superfluid simplicity itself. However, what you have created as your expression so far is structure, and you experience what you Are through this structure, in a variety of ways, often tight, restricting, holding in separate compartments. All are equally loved.

You are multiple in your structure, and until you have allowed all restriction to dissolve, you live in fragmentation within these forms.

They are a myriad movements of Being which stirred in you, in your lineage, in what you think you are. They have not yet completed the flow and remain in your universe, seeds waiting for their springtime. Notice when the first true breath of spring comes. Allow these energies to grow, develop, mature, become integrated. Allow all the movements of Being to live in you as a loving family.

Allow all your inner aspects and the poet and beloved strength of your soul to support you as you become One, in both awareness and experience.

3 April 2003

PADA 69
GATHERING

More than three years after I wrote the observations in BECOMING ONE - Pada 68, I find myself writing the following reflections after a session with a client, with a view to explaining a little.

There are no clients. I wonder sometimes how I have stayed sane in the intensity of my experience. Maybe I haven't!

I am the Heart consuming it all. I gave birth to the earth, and all her children. As did we all. Our own earth. But each in his or her own image and likeness. What is that likeness? What is a human system?

When you and I talk, or any two humans sit together for that matter, there are always more than two at the meeting. It can sometimes be like a gathering of unintegrated echoes. We each bring to the meeting or relationship a constellation of ghosts and frozen energies which have, to a greater or lesser degree, an autonomous life. However many of these '*pranas*', or breaths, we become aware of, there are always more unseen children in the wings waiting to be recognised and embraced consciously.

The strength of these echoes, and their ability to influence the conscious direction, varies according to the awareness of the 'individual' consciousness around whom they are constellated. Also the level of integration of the energy patterns and psychophysical imprints of their family dynamics, and the biological inheritance of their lineage. Our 'assignment' as consciousness is to consume these echoes, to be willing to let them in, embracing them, participants in a crazy, partying festival, dancing till dawn comes. And for us to be in all this celebration, moment by moment, breath by breath, simply the spontaneous, embodied life of the Heart.

An individual raised in an average family of unintegrated members can be a nation locked into one or several push-me pull-you civil wars, having inherited a tradition of terrorism and dissociation. He or she can become a continually integrating community, creating a team of cooperative allies and personalities with a range of skills and gifts moving towards self-actualisation and transcendence of the fragmented human condition. A cooperating humanity, an integrated earth, a whole universe.

Few are sufficiently aware yet to be able to recognise our state, except through, perhaps, the constant and misunderstood discomfort of inner or bodily warfare. Fewer still accept the challenge of minute-by-minute recognition and continual clearing of patterns and memory fragments, an absolutely essential process for potentially full-spectrum human beings choosing to live a life outside the box of default. The superfluity of casually produced material goods in much of the West, which are becoming increasingly more difficult to dispose of, is an out-picturing of these undigested ghosts, memory fragments and echoes.

What is a human system? It is a bundle of largely autonomous reflexes and patterns, half conscious, mostly unconscious. We appear as unintegrated memory complexes of habits and remnants of obsolete structures from our lineage. This continually rotating driver of the bus load of undigested echoes identifies with the experience of being the owner and director of itself, mistakenly believing it is one. This bundle of patterns of the false identity or memory complex is the vehicle through which consciousness is reflected to itself. Identification with this reflection is how these patterns on many different levels are perpetuated in consciousness. In this madness, we are inhabitants of Babel with no common language, except the silence of the Heart, like the undiscriminating stare of baby eyes, where for the most part we do not go for fear of death.

True Self, or Real Identity, is the central organising principle, a silent centrifugal force drawing all fragments to Itself, towards awareness, accepting and re-integrating these terrorist robotic ghosts in the system. It is the central Sun around which the echoing planets are constellated. True Self is the empty space, the Home, the no taste, no thing of the eastern scriptures. As this emptiness flows through, and as an integrating human system, it can seem to shine as the sun, a luminous dark radiance.

When the 'me and mine', this habitual fascination with the shadowy band of actors, begins to loosen, the experience of the empty Heart can give rise to a sense of being nothing but a depersonalised bundle of discordant but somehow familiar echoes. And as the Heart consumes these echoes, consuming is the same as loving them, being them, simply letting them live. They cannot die till they have lived. As the Heart consumes the unlived breaths and they die, it can be a devastating experience for the individual who is seemingly being wiped clean.

A void, like a death of everything we seemed to be. As can sometimes happen in primal experience or a massive, kundalini-type, energy reconfiguration. There are sometimes periods of intense disorientation, experiences of chaos and loss, as True Identity is established and identification with nothing in particular starts to be the case. It can be years before any functionality is established. In a few cases functionality does not appear to re-establish itself at all. Maybe as a race we have not yet lived long enough and in sufficient numbers to adapt to the emerging new life forms.

The New Life can seem unrecognisable from the former narrow perspective. If these new forms of life can be together like babies reflecting their naked, agenda-less state, they can ground the thread of New Life in joy. They are best served as consciousness when they are together shining on each other to reflect and magnify the vulnerable newness.

All our impulse for community is an out-picturing of this desire to experience the rhythm of our pre-existing wholeness in a simple dance. Desire for authentic communication and expression is the desire of the Heart of humanity to embrace all its children, and live in peace with Itself.

The word I have now is 'serviam', I will serve. It's like being available, available to Life. Living Alchemy.

The words of Lucifer, the light-bringer and antagonist, were 'non serviam'. I will not serve. It was only that arrogant, conscious attitude, which usually believes it is the one to be served! Ultimately there is only the play. All serves. Inevitably!

Many years ago I dreamt of being one of the Knights Templar dedicated to rebuilding the ruined holy places. As I write of it, it again touches my Heart. Rebuilding the temple.

I knew it was a call to restore the respect of the true holy place of the body, the Body of the Heart.

Sometime later I dreamt the bishop called me to be ordained as a priest. I know I was asking myself to commit to this process of gathering myself Home. The process is not out there among the people, though it may also seem to be so. The 'opus' is in the impeccable bending of the will, the lowering of the head to the ground, the surrender of the conscious attitude of one-sided ownership of this body. An alchemy of silent integration of the disparate elements of the so-called 'individual' human, and so transform the earth. It only takes One to free yourself, your family, your people, your earth, your universe.

"*The Spirit of the Lord is upon me, because he has anointed me to preach the good news to the poor. He has sent me to heal the broken-hearted, to proclaim release to the captives, recovering of sight to the blind, to deliver those who are crushed, and to proclaim the acceptable year of the Lord.*" Luke 4:18.

We are each the creator and the avatar of our own universe.

22 July 2006

PADA 70
FOSSIL FUEL

As we experience increasing clarity and direction in our lives, deliberate creation and focused precise intention become more and more the way to go.

We can choose to make a habit of beginning the day with some quiet time to reflect and create the intention for the day.

Being open to receive and enjoy all the beautiful expressions of love in form available for that day, all the flow and joy and feeling of 'already accomplished' gratitude inviting in an ever-increasing familiarity with being 24/7 in that feeling.

We can enjoy the excitement of realising that our thought and intention, our pictures and words on our inner vision board, are actually changing our experience!

We are each truly powerful!

As relaxation and peace, and intention to receive expressions of our joy, become established in a fresh habitual way of being, delightful surprises increasingly start to happen. The more we practise transmitting peace and gratitude, the more wellbeing and abundance begin to be our daily experience. So transmit gratitude 24/7.

As uncomfortable situations, events and feelings present themselves, we can become very practised at seeing these as fossil fuel to integrate, to put in the fire of the Heart to burn up and release new energy. The choice to see them in this way removes the habit of adding anxiety to the situation. Choosing to allow a new way enables us to relax, and accept that what is happening is a clearing process, and speeds up the integration. Sometimes gone in a flash! And straight back to transmitting clarity, peace and joyful anticipation of delightful events!

So, each day becomes a flow of receiving, swiftly clearing any fossil fuel you may find, and back to enjoying and playing with the energy of creation!

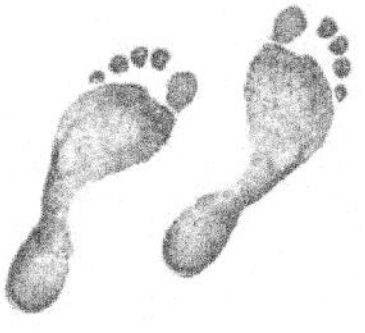

PADA 71
BE READY!

Some time after you declare to your universal field your intention to allow something into form, you begin to notice little signs that you have been heard, you have heard yourself!

This time depends on the amount of energy - love, excitement, pleasure - that you invest in what you want to create. Sometimes these signs which begin to show themselves are not perfect matches for what you are intending, but they are indications that something is beginning to emerge. A seed is beginning to sprout in the 'Field'. Maybe you want to manifest a new car, for example, but the ones you see are not quite right yet. Then you begin a process of being grateful for what is being brought to your attention, and at the same time refining precisely what you have declared. More clarity may be required. And more energy, which means more love, more pleasure at the thought of experiencing this.

Then maybe other more precise indications come. The right model, the right colour. Time for action maybe. Go and see some of them, take a test drive. Attend to your finances, be open to your new intention. So-called 'manifesting' is a precision skill which can be applied to bringing anything into form. When desire and allowing are perfectly matched, it can be instant. But **you** must play with it until you really get the hang of it.

Baby steps, and do some little thing towards it every day.

I remember one client years ago. She wanted a healing sanctuary in her back garden where she had a dirty old shed. She had no money. She cleared a tiny space among the rubbish, and put a white tissue, a tealight and a flower, and imagined. She would look at it and dream. She looked at ready-made wooden buildings, drew pictures, chose colours, and enjoyed the thought every day. A year later a beautiful fully- equipped healing room stood where the shed had been.

So, take action when the moment is right. Not too soon, but **be ready**! And watch for signs that the seed you planted is growing. No pushing. This causes resistance. Take action when the moment comes. It will then be smooth, simple and effortless. If not ready yet, find more love and clarity, and practise bringing this thought to birth, and being in the stillness.

It is a precise art, mind and Heart together, clearing resistance and magnifying the flow...

PADA 72
FEELING

When we focus on creating a flow of thankfulness and enjoyment, that frequency is what we transmit. The genie, the unconscious, picks up on the **feeling** to tell it what you are putting attention on, and what you want more of. The **feeling** is the marker which signals 'this way', 'choose me'! Often we let our feelings run, a bit hit-and-miss, in reaction to circumstances which we have not deliberately, consciously, chosen.You really can **choose** the feeling you want to broadcast, just as you choose the music you play. When you put that strong feeling together with what you **do** desire, you communicate deliberately with that part of your unconscious mind which creates your experiences.

Love all the little and big things you can. Spend a few minutes being thankful, creating a high-frequency transmission through your body.Do nice things for your body. Wear lovely colours. Do things you enjoy. Pretend to be playing when you feel you 'have to' do things you think you don't want to do. Perhaps keep a journal of the things you love. Feel grateful for what you're enjoying. Play and see what happens, and share it as that increases the effect!

PADA 73
YOU

You, who you really are, prior to this bodymind, beneath your story and every thought you may have about your life.

You are the one you are always in relationship with, in union, beyond relationship.

So it is essential to be curious about that! How could I know and experience this freedom more fully?

You shine through every relationship. You are that one that Rumi refers to in his poetry:

"One look from you and I see you in everything
looking back at me
Those eyes in which all things live and burn."

What is it that we are experiencing when we don't appear to know this self-evident fact? When we don't always notice the bliss and abundance of our being?

This effect is brought about by the movement of Being, moving through old structure, ancient, incomplete communication, unfinished beliefs and thoughts. We can become aware of this, and allow these archaeological remnants to dissolve in the light of our choice. There is no other! And we have the opportunity of fresh experience. There is the most enormous tenderness in experiencing shadow and distortion.when we receive it softly, with curiosity.

The Dyad Heart Communication process is an amazingly powerful and practical way to explore the experience, this knowing and this choice to recognise no other. Only One. To know the true Self.

Once you have learnt the Heart Communication process and the simple way of being still and silent while listening, allowing **all** the space for the other to express and be drawn ever deeper into their own unravelling, it becomes a fast track to awakening and freedom.

And this is what this life is about! Untangling! Allowing the veils through which we see our world, the filters of our conditioning, and echoes of the past, to be dissolved.

In the Heart Communication process we have the chance to experience and practise being in this state with 'others', and we prepare to take that curiosity back into the story of our life.

We can explore 'relationship' on all levels, but exploring 'shadow' relationship and how it serves us in awakening, and withdrawal of projection, is especially valuable.

Be curious to see that 'You' which Rumi speaks of in everyone you meet and think about today. Place your hand on your Heart and ask to see **who** and **what** this really is. Especially when it feels challenging to see!

PADA 74
QUANTUM HEART

The Quantum Heartspace adds a whole new dimension of functionality to the human story. The vision of the mystics and quantum functionality. It is a dimension where we are in instant communication. Where the dimensions of time and space are transcended. When the Eye of the Heart opens, we see and experience **who** and **what** is truly present, as well as the temporarily modified vehicle of expression that living presence appears as, in the physical realm.

This has the often instantaneous effect of softening or dissolving the experience of separation and distorted perception, and sharpening the ability of the mind, and body, to function optimally.

This whole physical realm is a collusive perception, a 24/7 virtual reality, magic show, and is, in any case, infinitely customisable. We know time and space are simply the dimensions of the box which encloses the mind. Quantum physics tells us this is so, but our experience, for the most part, has told us otherwise. But we all have flashes of experience which show us something different.

We can live in the superfluid state. We are able to vibrate with such clarity that we activate that state in others. On the physical dimension we seem to acquire enhanced abilities of perception. Seeing things from multiple points of view. And enabling others to see too. Our perception expands from single particle perception to include that of the wave, and multiple particles.

Practising seeing and communicating in this way, being **together** in this way, at my events, retreats and small dyad groups, and in our 'little personal' life, leads eventually to stabilisation in this dimension, this field of expanded awareness and enhanced ability. Seeing and being seen for what we truly are, we draw that way of being into form.

Experiencing and recognising this communion we create a *sangha,* a virtual community of the Heart. Creation happens by distinguishing one possibility from all others, and choosing to energise this way of being.

While remaining aware of the distorted habitual fragmented perception of the mind and our previous programming, we, the emerging community of the Heart, individually and collectively, begin to radiate this brilliant vision, this enhanced hologram of the unity of the Quantum Heart, the 'way we choose to see'. It becomes an ever more stable Reality. Eventually becoming the default way of perceiving! Distortion of any kind is not Real! As you see it, so it is! Choose to make it your experience

In each of our lives it only takes **one** to be in communion, rather than in communication. It is ultimately an effortless choice to see that faint light of the Heart. By contemplation the light it is energised, it becomes brighter, clearer. We create a stronger battery.

When we contemplate that light in the midst of confusion and muddled perception, we attract others who also love to see in that way. Your choice?

The world reconfigures naturally around us. And eventually stabilises in the way we choose to experience it. The effect in the everyday world is what we call miraculous. But it is a natural effect.

It only takes one, but the hologram is stronger as more are drawn to see what I can see! The natural state of resonance.

All this is no longer a distant vision of the stars, but is accessible now. We are the doorways to the enhanced life of the Quantum Heart.

Humanity is already stirring. We can activate and ground that new vision, opening to the power of the Heart. It is now essential. It is time.

2 April 2009

PADA 75
FIRE IN THE HEART

"The stone that was rejected shall become the cornerstone of the temple." – Psalm 118:22

This paradox is the integration of the shadow. The inclusion of all wounded, damaged rejected, seemingly unlovable. Loving the unloved.

Rahu is paradox.

Inclusion of the disabled, unwanted, unlovable.

This is the restoration of the temple.

The valleys are filled, and the mountains laid low.

I am come to bring the good news to the poor, to comfort the broken-hearted and make the lame to walk, the blind to see.

I am come to set fire to this world, light a blaze in the Heart… And behold, it is already alight and blazing.

Shakti, shakti, shakti.

Lightning, power, fire!

The tsunami of the Heart Waves.

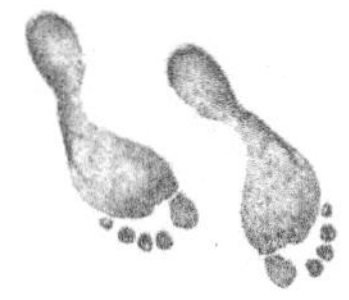

PADA 76
LIFE IS A LITTLE SONG

Life is movement, a precious, flowing, feeling tenderness, a continual pouring of Self into form, playing in loving expression!

Life is a little song that Nature is singing to herself! That is what we are here for... to be 'divine life artists' in the Global X Factor!

Nature does just this, revealing herself in shape and pattern and colour, living newness, spontaneous entertainment, always and everywhere…

Kishori Devi

PADA 77
LET THERE BE LIGHT

"I experience myself as two cells, one from my mother's body and one from my father, merging in an amazing nuclear fusion of light forming the world of my body."

This experience is described by a participant at one of my many *Stargate of Birth* events, and is a cellular memory akin to *"Let there be Light"* in the book of Genesis. We each incarnate into our own unique life movie through our own Stargate of light and sound.

Living with this awareness facilitates the release of identification with our current story, freeing us to be simply present as the true Self.

Among the many disciplines that I researched in my early exploration of body and consciousness are both somatic regression and enlightenment mastery.

The experience of the *Stargate of Birth* can activate a profound realisation of who and what we really are, our True Identity.

PADA 78
DARKNESS

Darkness invites us to explore the unseen, the unknown, the unexpected, and its role in the evolutionary process.

What is Shadow?

Fear, the unknown, the 'dark forces', the beast, the *atithi*, the unexpected, that which stops us in our tracks, cutting right across the conscious direction? Chaos, disaster, terrorism, abuse, loss, death, including our own?

What is our relationship with our own perceived inability to be all we might consciously choose to be?

What does it mean to have compassion for ourselves?

How do we allow integration of what we would prefer not to happen?

What can be our attitude towards the seemingly unthinkable, seemingly robotic chaos in our lives and the larger world, the apparently valueless events that some might call evil?

What is our relationship with the so-called saboteur, accidents, mistakes, disasters?

How can we really love and accept our weakness, surrender control? Of what relevance is it to welcome the *atithi*, the unexpected, and often unwelcome, guest at the table of our life, with tenderness, humility and compassion?

What is the living relevance of the fairy tale of Beauty and the Beast?

What part do resistance and inertia play in our life?

Darkness is **newness**, the unseen and as yet unknown and ungrown.

PADA 79
FALLOUT

From the first big bang of cellular merging in nuclear fusion, our whole experience of life in a body is totally predictable.

We can predict fallout patterns from explosions.

Our life is a predictable fallout pattern, as we see in astrology.

We are on automatic default to live out our life until we awaken to remember what we are, embrace our destiny and choose live it consciously, on purpose.

"Until you make the unconscious conscious, it will rule your life and you will call it Fate." – Carl Jung

What are you choosing?

PADA 80
HERE EXISTS

THIS embraced IS reality
A streaking comet
A sweet speck of stardust
In all its shining loveliness

A ribbon of music
A flame of living water
Shimmering in this vast emptiness
A fleeting floater in the eye of what I am

Drifting to the secret shore
Of the Eyeland of the Heart
I leave my boat where quiet ripples lap the sand
The evening tide turns

At the edge of the ocean
The silent darkness calls me
Drawing me down as a lover
To rest in depths of unspeakable stillness

An exquisite stream of nectar flows….
Oozing drops of golden juice
Maya opens her ever virgin Heart
Falling softly drunken into the deep.

PADA 81
OUR TREASURE

My aim in all the group events and individual sessions I hold exploring the Shadow and Living on Purpose is to serve the unique perspective of the One awakening as the apparent 'individual,' by facilitating awareness and understanding of the human condition, enabling ever-increasing insight into how we seem to live, only half alive, actually living with the brakes on!

I love sharing ways of seeing and embracing 'these bugs in the system', these 'barriers' which prevent us from experiencing our true nature. These 'bugs' are always, in fact, moments of opportunity, calling us to make a choice for what we really want. Rahu invitations to allow more of what we are to grow.

I love to show how we already have and are a treasure we can attend to, and enhance. Attention is not something we have to go searching for. For me it is not in a mystical 'spiritual' life beyond, but always at hand in a very ordinary, intimate way.

I love to create motivation to give attention to what is Real, awakening us to realise, make real, the Reality of who and what we actually are, unlimited, abundant, playful, childlike lovebliss, in our complete energy and power, 360-degree full spectrum life, here and now, in all the tiniest details of our everyday life, each in our unique impulse to express and create moment by moment.

Together we can create this freedom to be. Let's go for it!

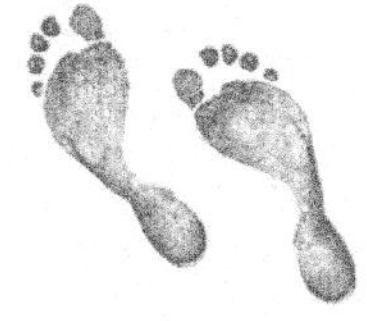

PADA 82
OPEN YOUR EYES

We have one thing to do now, to open our eyes, to realise that we make it all up. We made our little story up, layer on layer, and now we can ask for the key to release ourselves from the insanity. I offer training for this, a treasure house of information and simple direct playful processes, methods for this release, expansion and empowerment.

The training is a twofold process, like breathing, emptying and filling, stillness and movement, dying and birthing.

Firstly, we begin by noticing resistance, and inviting the apparently closed door to open:

Allowing, discovering, embracing, revising, digesting, releasing the distortion of old structure, old outdated programmes of perception and behaviour.

Naturally we come to realise that we have brought everything into form, as God does in the story of Genesis after the creation of the world. *"Behold it is very good"*. Like a child include everything; especially what the mind says is not good, not enough! And then rest.

When emotions are in turmoil or mind criticises, we can simply give attention to what is Real. This naturally increases flow, and the unreal dissolves and fades from our experience. It dies from lack of energy, and the released life force now fuels the fire of the Real.

And secondly, in the inner silence which now remains:

Creation, active birthing of new form, nurturing the seeds, creating baby holoforms of your Heart's desires, seeing no difference between personal and impersonal desires, proactive building in alignment with what we love, the blueprint of the Heart. Allowing the natural flow of abundant Real life to come into our experience, with ever-increasing refinement and delight.

We have a huge variety of simple practical tools available for the clearing and the creation processes. Many paths, many focusing tools, none is better than any other. It is what you love and are spontaneously drawn to in the moment, which is the way for you. Here you will find a wealth of treasure from which to select. Go with what you love, and enjoy!

Some ways you may already be aware of, some are available freely on the internet. Some are recreated when we meet to support the conscious intention to be free.

Using them consistently, giving attention, with intention and commitment, activates the power to serve you. Reading and thinking about the ways does not do it.

Remember, to straighten the crooked, which is the common idea of 'healing', you must first straighten yourself! Are you ready to make that choice? To let yourself remember that nothing out there is crooked! Absolutely Nothing!

Are you willing to allow yourself to straighten, to align to your blueprint and to release your whole self, without exception, from your silent accusation?

All disturbing effects and emotions arise from our collusive maintenance of the illusion. 'Emotion' means moving out from your centre, and is quite different from your feeling. Emotions are there to show you what you have erroneously believed and created.

Release your illusory dreamlife and allow your Real creative life to unfold now!

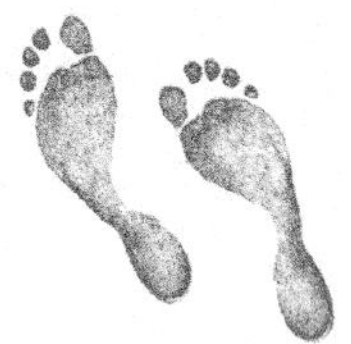

PADA 83
SCRATCHING THE ITCH

The process of integration and accelerating evolution that is currently occurring is experienced as a fusion of two energetic flows. One is a vast, impersonal, spontaneous, powerful outpouring, a Niagara Falls, and the other is the 'unreal' energy of confinement and apparent ownership which defines and contains and shapes and imagines itself accountable. To whom can it be accountable?

The unconditioned and the conditioned are both present at the same time. As the two currents flow together, the turbulence of the two currents swirling together is experienced. The shaping energy is widened and stretched, and moves with the power of the outpouring of the first flow.

I am not here to satisfy unfulfilled needs and wants as if you were still babies, to scratch your itch, so to speak. I am here to wake you up to what you already are. Like Hanuman, forgetful of his immortality, wandering on the shores of Bharat, you too can jump to Lanka with one leap. You have dreamed the technology for awakening, but you may still be blind to who you really are, the One immortal consciousness awakening in form.

These so-called needs and wants are not yet true desire in form. They are a sucking in of a reversed energy flow, a black hole, and unreal. I am here to show how responding fully to true desire causes a flow of such energetic magnitude that needs and wants which come from an incorrect energy flow melt away like mist in the morning sun. It is not, however, for you to ignore them and vainly hope that they will disappear. They are signs of rivers of emotional energy in your inner landscape which you can track to their source to find the false belief and reframe it, reversing the flow to become real desire.

I am here to show how the crenellations and contours of the inner landscape are reflected on the screen of this world as the hills and valleys of your life, in the same way as the shadows on the walls of Plato's cave. I am here to show you how, layer by layer, pixel by pixel, you constructed this inner landscape. I am here to cause these frozen and barren landscapes to flow again, that the valleys may be filled and the hills levelled and the desert blossom as the rose.

5 June 2006

PADA 84
TREASURE TRAIL

Our life is **literally** a 24/7 treasure trail. We each set up a master game plan for ourselves on coming into this world. And we each put all the ingredients for a fantastic game into a unique blueprint. I offer ways to use the design tools you have at your disposal to customise your own treasure map.

Our outer adventures in this world are a faithful replica of our inner landscapes. You can find and decipher the clues on your own treasure trail. The good news is that there is a way to make your results more consistent with what you want to find.

The huge joke is that you **always** find what you look for!

And choosing to go along the road less travelled, and the way you enjoy, really are the true paths.

I would like to share some of the secrets of my trail blazing with you, which may make it easier for you to find the clues which literally lead to both your own inner and outer treasure.

Most of us spend years wandering about here and there, wondering how to live. What am I here for? What shall I do? Where am I going? Finding clues and the paths which lead to treasure, but often seeming to go round in circles and down potholes.

All a bit hit-and-miss! We come equipped with a series of templates, and a few maps based on these templates that others have used.

We create our own unique map and we hide the treasure where we want to, and then we forget where we have buried it!

3 June 2006

PADA 85
OUR INNER TEAM

We have to engage **all** the members of our inner team, our inner family, to find the clues and retrace the paths to find the treasure on our treasure trail.

We can develop a whole range of skills to fully engage in this adventure of life. Inner team building, or integration of all our aspects, including, most essentially, the aspects that we don't spontaneously seem to enjoy, and which we think we would be better off without! Members of our Rahu team! Our beloved opponent.

The team has to get on together in perfect flow to enjoy and benefit from the challenges.

All the people in your life and your mind are, without exception, faithful reflections of aspects of you which you need to fully solve the clues.

You also have team members you don't know much about yet, genies and fairy godmothers, angels and power animals, and so much more. Team members who require your attention in order to grow into their full power.

There are templates for integrating the current players in your game, and templates for magical living, templates of the shadowlands, and templates to create a full spectrum team, and more. From them you can customise your own high-resolution maps for terrain you may be temporarily traversing.

3 June 2006

PADA 86
THE INNER LANDSCAPE

On our treasure trail, orienteering and map-reading of our inner landscape are other skills we require.

Each of us designs our own inner landscape, with rivers and jungles and dark forests, and challenging adventures constructed from our own unique set of coordinates. Often we don't dare to set out into the unknown jungles on the edges of our usual routes; we prefer to keep to well-lit areas. We don't dare to go deeper.

We can learn tracking skills about how to read and follow the flow of emotions to their source in our inner landscape. Are your rivers stagnant swamps, or dried up channels? Are there rapids and waterfalls? What are the beliefs which lie at their root? Do they flow from melting glaciers, or spring from deep in the earth? It is literally a jungle to explore.

You can consciously create your own game plan. You can discover which templates are in your current inner software, and replace them at will. It takes patience and skill to begin this, but the good news is you can learn to draw clear maps, and when you do, remember that you **always** find what you are searching for!

So, design your own map. Customise it by deciding what you really want.

I desired stability, which didn't come and go. What do you desire?

3 June 2006

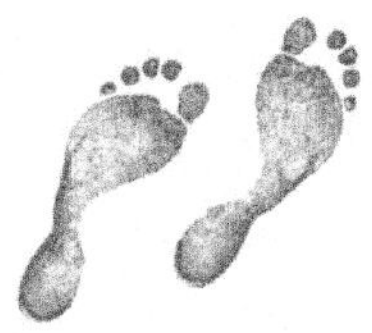

PADA 87
LIFE IS FRACTALINE

You are powerful! You are abundance!

Whatever you focus on grows and blossoms… like a seed, with water and sunshine.

The energy of your attention and your thoughts are sunshine, and life comes alive through you.

You are powerful, far more than you can imagine. Life is fractaline. It expands wherever you look. Your imagination is a touchstone, an Aladdin's lamp. You are focus. You are attention.

How are you using your focus?

Conscious creation is what the 'I' that is 'we' is here for. Together we can create the world anew. Together you can replace old collective beliefs which create the world you currently experience. Embracing all we already are, and joining with the unknown, the new, is the way.

Poverty and lack are absences. They are 'unreal'. We don't need to put attention on the absences.

What will you choose to energise?

Abundance is our true nature. In that knowledge anything is possible.

Are you following the impulse to join in dreaming abundance for all?

You are the creator of your reality, and life is yours to form.

Life is shapable. She responds to our thoughts.

Your thoughts and feelings create the world.

Our world. Your world.

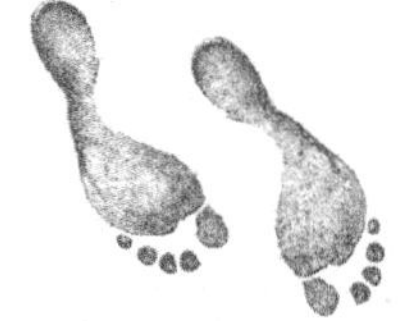

PADA 88
EVENING ON A BEACH IN INDIA

The wet sand is like a mirror reflecting purple, orange, silver, pink, bubbles of white foam water like silk in the evening sea. Incredible fairytale sky, like polished silver.

"What is your country?" a curious voice asks. "Please, one photo."

Streaks of burnt orange, green and violet. My shadow is a haze of purple stretching down the river bank behind me.

On the cliff top earlier the sea was a rainbow, deep violet, a rim of luminous green right at the edge. Fineness of pastels and watercolours. Colours impossible to describe. Violet, grey and flame, orange, pink and purple. Breathtaking sky.

Colours fading from orange to pale crimson. Razor-edge layers surrounding the earth. Spectacular display, this is all my beauty. The world sits in my Heart, as a little walnut in the hand of Julian of Norwich. Silver mist rising from the water now.

Towards dusk the waves start to toss. White water sprays and tumbles at my feet, and the waves catch at my toes and soak my legs to my knees. I sit back on the sand in the evening light and wait for darkness.

All of a sudden I am surrounded by hordes of curious children. One very articulate little girl tells me her name is Ashwiniraj. She asks me lots of questions. A *pujari* in a white *dhoti* sits on the sand nearby, a square red cloth spread in front of him full of sticks of incense and ghee, items for evening *puja*. Ashwiniraj brings her elder brother and a younger one, and her wild little sister, one by one to meet me.

I relish the moment in contemplation of light and dark.

PADA 89
NAUSEA

How to describe what my experience is, and what I am knowing? This whole existence is as insubstantial as a painting on clouds.

Past, present, future, here and there are simply points of reference in a multidimensional virtual image. The past can be changed as easily as the future by one who sees how. *"Give me a fulcrum and I will move the world,"* says Archimedes. And I also heard he said, *"Give me a paintbrush and I will paint the universe."*

I live everywhere at once. This body contains the codes for the universe. Is the coding. It is not a comfortable knowing these days. I am not interested in these shadows. Insubstantial ghosts and echoes. No desire for anything arises. It is a virtual mind-created playground. Stuffed with overwhelm. Anything is possible, and I do not dream the newness. Inertia is my experience right now.

I dream distantly of simplicity. Emptiness. White walls. Green freshness. A paperless silence with white butterflies and tiny waterfalls.

PADA 90
DYING TO THE OLD SELF

What you are in Reality, in your core, is absolute **simplicity**. What you are potentially, in this world, is full-spectrum, radiant expression of this simplicity.

You are literally a star, outflowing and shining in every aspect of life as an infinitely unfolding source of curious delight. This simplicity has been tasted, intuited, experienced by many, spoken of by some, embodied by a few - masters, teachers, mystics, little children. Some call it love. This is just a word, a finger pointing at the moon, as Osho said.

The destiny of the 'individual', if they allow it, is to embody that potential, to allow that simple Reality to shine. To become Real. Once we allow Reality to replace the old structures and restrictions through which the average human limps along, then Real Life can become fully functional in every area.

And that Reality, while the underlying consciousness is the same in all, is as unique in its individual expression as a fingerprint. To allow the fossil fuel of our old structure to be consumed and transformed takes willingness, courage and commitment to a process of Self-Inquiry, undoing and rebirth. This is alchemy. Dying to the old self.

For this alchemy to take place, the familiar structures of life, the way we have lived, the understanding of what life is, even, must dissolve. A revolution takes place; this dissolution of former personal life can feel like death, and complete bewilderment. It seems now, for many, to no longer be a conscious choice, but simply what is happening. The tide of Living Reality is rising spontaneously, overwhelming the lives of many. This life, this dream, which arise for the spontaneous delight of Being, seemingly become a battleground of dysfunctionality, distortion. Money, relationship, divorce, separation, food, health, fear, emotional balance, sex, abuse, loss, death, survival…

The question arises of how to live, now? How to be simply the unresisting delight in the moment, while the consuming of the old strategic way is taking place? How to gracefully let go and be reborn? How to allow 'you' to be updated into the moment, and fulfil the potential of being fully alive? To evolve into a continuously integrating, fully functioning expression of life, radiantly alive in the moment and responding truly and gracefully in every area of your life?

13 May 2003

PADA 91
RECEIVING

One of the essential pieces of the jigsaw of so-called 'manifesting' is practising **receiving**. When the flow is smooth and the major distortions of our conditioning are integrated, this is not a block! However, many have been taught it is "*more blessed to give than to receive.*" When, in fact, giving and receiving are two sides of the same coin.

There is no Other. When you give unconditionally, you give to yourself! Dreaming, visioning, clearing, expressing current feeling and stagnant emotion, gratitude and appreciation, disclosing, grounding, staying true, high self-love and care, surrendering to the Heart in the midst of challenges. All these, and more, are of infinite value.

However, practising receiving is a crucial aspect of the process. Spend five minutes once a day, or even twice a day, sitting silently, hands on your knees with palms facing up. Practise experiencing the flow of the abundance of the Universe! Where giving and receiving are one. I encourage you to begin to journal your experience now. It is a fast path to integration and awakening. All for one and one for all!

PADA 92
WILD

1st June

Went to Dorothy to develop the Rahu production with her. Instead I read her my poem *My Ocean Mind* (see page 39), and I burst. Overflowed. Cried for an hour. I can see it is time to give up living through others, however good I am at it. Time to stop hiding. But I feel very, very scared.

2nd June

I wake this morning without the feeling of dread. Though very regressed. The house is the biggest tip ever. I no longer pick anything up. I don't know where anything is.

I bought some wine yesterday, and one bottle last week. I don't normally drink alcohol, but I have gone beyond knowing what I want. I can just be here, at least for a few days, and see what evolves. It has to be a whole new way of living, and I don't yet know how to get there.

How am I to live in this unreal world?

PADA 93
EXTRAORDINARILY ORDINARY

The therapist appears to exert an unnecessarily enormous amount of pressure on my physical body, causing an inordinate level of pain. What unconscious force is he masking for me? My own desire to experience my own pressure, to externalise the inner forces? To feel the impulse to flow, which has built up and has not been allowed expression?

In the last session we spoke of the core issue. It seems that I was born with weakened kidneys. One very damaged, the other ready to give up. I almost died, he says. One of the functions of the kidneys is to support the liver. My kidneys had little strength or life force, were not up to the job. Forced to eat, especially milk and dairy products, my body didn't want what it didn't have the resources to process.

At three and a half years old in the springtime (in a phone call my mother remembered maybe four and a half) I got the measles. Before the measles I was very thin, and didn't want to eat. After the illness I began to eat. In anger, my body appeared to give up resistance, surrendering to my mother's iron will. My liver began to attempt something for which it had no support, and went into self-destruct. I obeyed her insistent demand for obedience, for perfection, with resentment, and I internalised the rage, the relentless need to control. This dynamic she did not, could not, process and integrate, even with her best will. Instead she allowed her body to be controlled by doctors and surgeons, who cut out the collapsing bits for her, in order to relieve her agonising experience of emotional, physical and environmental pressure.

The baton of integration was handed to me. The emotional and physical pain I have experienced in my life have been almost unbearable, but the suffering I witnessed my mother endure, especially when she was younger, was exquisite torture. To me she was a martyr and a dragon, and brilliantly creative. I admired her ability to make anything with perfection. I avoided the rigid control as best I could, the unbending iron discipline, and what seemed to me to be unkind. She did always what she thought was right, and was very generous to me later in life when I had the children, and when I got sick.

I cannot say I felt very close to her when I was young, although in later years I realised I was, in an intensely symbiotic way. In her own way, as she got older, she became more aware that acceptance was necessary, and so dealt with as much as she was able through prayer and her Catholic faith. In her old age she appeared to come to periods of contentment, of quiet oases and simple enjoyment of what remained to her, her love of garden design and grandchildren filling her life. At the end we had both begun to mellow.

It was my turn to hit the jackpot of our family's savings! To take on the accumulated, internalised suffocating rage, the counterpole of the conscious goodness, Christian patience, stoical endurance and obedience to pretended male superiority that I saw often ran like a thread through the lives of some of the women in families around me.

Later in my life I realised that women's true opinion of men differed enormously from the surface set-up. To me, men often seemed to be hollow, weak, apparently domineering cardboard cut-out figures, sorely in need of protection. Probably from overwhelming feminine rage at their not coming up with the goods, at not seeming to be what their women desired them to be. In reality they did not know how to be, any more than the women did. Everything seemed to be based on this mutual robotic collusion.

When I looked at these men with my inner eye they crumbled with the fragile consistency of Maltesers.

PADA 94
THE MAGICAL SUPERFLUID STATE

The magical superfluid state of flow into form. Beyond personal doing lies the flow of true giving and receiving.

The energy of what is called **giving**, of outpouring, is very sweet. It is a living flow in the moment. Openness calls this flow into being; allows this pouring of love into form. The energy of this flow is the innate movement of love made visible and tangible. The innocence of a baby draws it irresistibly from a mother's heart. Choiceless surrender, without insistence on the outcome, generates selflessness in the heart.

Nature flows with abundance, making no demands on which of its seeds grow or die. In truth, there is no giving. What looks like giving is the spontaneous response of being love, of allowing. The greater the surrender, the acceptance, the more the superfluid state of total flow comes into being, this state which melts the very earth and moves even mountains.

All this flow of nature is immediately negated the moment there is any insistence. The more insistent the demand, the tighter grows the restriction on the flow into form. A harsh demand, or a pleading based on error in the mind, or victim consciousness, closes down this magical sweetness. The more begging, the greater becomes the experience of poverty and lack. Error and imbalance produce more error and imbalance. Any giving which savours of strategy and doing is equally limited.

Fortunately these states of mind are temporary modifications in this relative world, and the law of love is not limited to this world of appearances. Love, abundance, will always flow where and when it spontaneously enjoys, in spite of limited human consciousness. All form is the flow of divine expression, and carries within itself the seeds for full unfolding of the infinite wonder, the magical garden of paradise, without limit, at all times.

What passes for 'spiritual life' or 'religion' is so often a limitation of this law. Life is always pouring into all of its expressions everything that is 'needed' for the enjoyment of the whole play. Nothing is ever required from any other form as I am ALL there is. All form is intrinsically empty, and no apparent form can supply the seeming 'needs' of another.

My beloved India is a case in point, with its custom of honouring the 'higher nature' of gurus, revering the greater deservingness of those who are apparently more 'spiritual' than others. "All is Me! There is no other. No higher, no lower, no richer, no poorer. Only the flow of love-pleasure in to and out of form. So, no strategic giving! No giving in order to accomplish anything. Just follow the impulse of the Heart, which is also your personal impulse.

The energy of payment is very different. This has nothing to do with the magical power of love. Payment is simply a contract at the surface level between two parties, an exchange of energy, time, goods or money, for time, goods, or services received in this world of appearances.

The magic of flow can, of course, happen anyway, anywhere, anytime, because love is not limited. However, flow is usually experienced as restricted in these exchanges because of the imposition of the tight structure of expectation. Contracts at the surface level are not usually the place for the highest demonstration of the flow of love.

When two or three people willingly join in a project following the spontaneous impulse of the Heart in the **now**, without thoughts of personal gain, but simply allowing the outpouring of love everywhere, the ground is prepared for miracles. And the results of these miracles flower and fruit, and continue to flower and fruit infinitely.

PADA 95
SUCCESS

Dull, dull, dull
Dank, grey, aching rawness,
smoothed and tucked under this plastic wrapping,
spilling fat maggots, oozing through the
perforations.

Failure shivers, trembles, gathering, birthing to a
ripeness, Bursts a swollen follicle.

My success is this exquisite pain, rising to a roar, a
tsunami racing in my blood.

25 October 2009

PADA 96
KALI MA

Awareness rebels impatient, violent
A squirming mass of ancient dust
Awakening embodied in tender disturbance
Patterns of sucking emptiness pouring streaming
from her squalid flaccid breasts
Spirals of cactus shards poised to penetrate the
breathing spaces
In crazed bones
Suspended by spider thread above yawning abyss
extending from nothing to nowhere

She is Kali. Black wanton oozing overflowing
sexual wild
A necklace of skulls adorning her disintegrating
form;
Eating and drinking despair, slices of her mother's
sick body in cakes and ale
Tall wispy boney fingers wrapped in tree mirage,
beckon waving mistily across the blue hazed
horizon

Voices pleading now among the garbage and the
flowers.

Mother, mother, mother... Show us the way out of this box
Lead us out of the stinking morass, through the cracks in this world maze
Set us free from this slimy, crawling, chocolate-boxing, electric shocking,
searing smearing tenderness that we are. Is there no one? No hand to hold
No sweet skin to sniff in all this putrid isolation?

This mazing, mad mazed, maggoty mind, rippling pustule-filled, syrup on shit?
"Oh what can ail thee knight-at-arms, alone and palely loitering
The sedge hath withered from the lake and no birds sing"

Raw nails jabbing stabbing, abandoning the computer keys,
screaming raging disappointed harpies denied their holocaust
Ohhh creator mind makes heaven, creator mind makes hell.
Echoing shards of paradise lost.
I never promised you a rose garden sings the Heart.

But here is one thorn and the burning ghats of
destruction
A journey of rotten fruit of chaotic fractaline
unreason.
One by one SHE, the mad one, diligently plucks the
rank threads of time from her shining skull.

Kishori Jeanette McKenzie

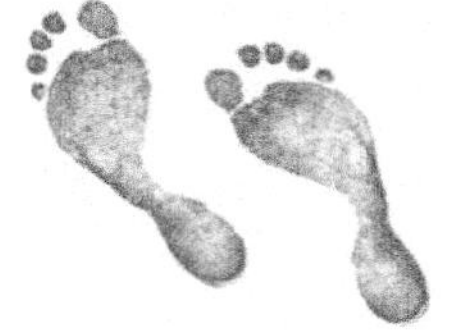

PADA 97
FREE OF TIME

There is a process of awakening occurring. Stirring. Growth of humanity into authenticity, the authentic pulsating Real Life of this present moment, originating before and beyond space-time.

Realising fully the mechanism by which we create, by perception, this world in which we seem to exist. Becoming fully alive. Here-now is inside what 'this I that is we' truly is.

They call it *kundalini,* rising of the feminine, the goddess. Naming it makes it comforting to the mind which wants a handle on it.

It is what Teilhard de Chardin called the omega point. I see this as the converging of two parallel existences, two parallel lines, seemingly unable to meet. They do meet, they have already rejoined. The gap is closed. There is no gap. It produces ecstasy in my body as I write this. The kingdom of heaven is all about you. There is no separation between time-bound existence and eternity. Eternity is not some unending stretch of time. It has nothing to do with time. I/we am already full spectrum presence. This body is the *antakarana,* the rainbow bridge.

The bridge exists as this body. I have descended into hell and been at peace there, and am rising. I am conscious now of the path of return.

All 'things' required for this story are now being provided. I am alive. I am that Living One who is writing the story! Houses, people, money. What are these to the script writer!

This is a natural evolutionary process. Apparently turning ourselves inside out. Akin to the biology of birth. Shedding the unreality of all *vasana, samskaras,* as a huge carapace, an amniotic sac. The vast majority of forms are still walking automaticities, entombed in the past. Archaeological specimens.

In this body I am engaged in alchemy, this process of gathering, absorbing shadow, transmuting and freeing it, accumulating generations of archaeology and digesting the alchemical nigredo. I am consuming what I have embodied as myself, as this body. Like the pelican feeding its young on its blood.

We are updating, moving from space-time-based life to infinity-eternity, enabling us to choose to become fully awakened luminaries, a fully awakened luminous community of light. My body is a virus in consciousness. Catalytic. Nuclear fusion, Heart expansion... The picture is so vast, it is almost impossible to convey it.

Humanity is transmuting. It is the next phase, and there is no personal ownership. This is a device to facilitate embodiment. All is one. A field of conscious awareness, arising with a natural destiny of evolution.

We are allowing this unfolding step-by-step. Growing a tree from a seed. We are shedding the past carapace like a snake sheds its skin. To be born into life free of time and entropy.

7 October 2010

PADA 98
CATALYTIC ENCOUNTERS

This living bodymind is your touchstone, your prima materia, your crucible, your Aladdin's lamp, your open sesame, your key to the more of you, your doorway to your genius, your genie giant, your power, the alchemist's gold. All of these and none of these. Everything is the silent face of the Beloved.

Your embodiment is the doorway to merging with your mind box, so you may truly see it, encompass it and transcend it. It is your way to know and embody the ONE you truly are.

Your body is a multi-layered coat of many colours, a multi-dimensional universe... There exist a multiplicity of healing modalities and bodyworks, from Feldenkrais to Craniosacral, from massage to Rolfing. The list is endless.

When realisation dawns that you, the conscious embodied living I, not the selected method or practitioner, is the way: that you, a consciousness not distinct from the consciousness of the apparent practitioner, are the cause, then an encounter with a 'practitioner/therapist' can become a catalytic superfluid moment, an adventure of merging, exploration, and unfolding for both apparent 'giver' and 'receiver'.

When you accept that the truth is that you do not get anything, and you do not give anything, but you simply allow and witness the never-ending story of unfolding. Then for practitioner or client, for lover or beloved, what we call healing, therapy or love-making, is simply a magical moment of merging. It is potentially a voyage of discovery, an adventure and unfolding of the embodiment. Senses, mind, intuition, will, feeling, knowing, everything.

The strategy of putting your attention on an apparent problem, with a view to finding a solution, is part of the old paradigm. Radical wholeness, realigning to the infinite blueprint that you are, comes in the moment of release into the no mind, into that superfluid state which moves mountains.

PADA 99
IMPECCABLE DISCIPLINE

Sunday 7 am, 1 October

I am performing *samyama* like Patanjali, on everything.

On every circumstance of my life, on every organ, on every cell, on every breath. Every breath of the body has to relax back into the Heart, in every moment. It is an impeccable discipline.

This exploration of my bodymind is *samyama*. It is useless unless it is complete curious neutral exploration from the Heart. Neutral is not cold, but has an enquiring feeling and attention. Ecstatic (out of the mind), as opposed to strategic.

Planning must be without emotional attachment to the outcome.

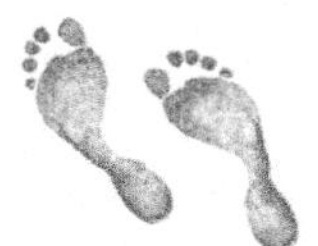

PADA 100
YOUR CAPPED OIL WELL

It is practical enlightenment we require, here and now. Choosing to experience the wonder in every moment. Clearing and reclaiming the swamps of negative emotion. The earth has been stripped of our trees of fruit and resting places. The land of our bodies expresses toxicity and lack, confusion, the dryness of minds discussing enlightenment. Heart and the body are sources of living water and nourishment. It is the state of alienation, seeking for solutions, that is the occasion for the imaginary plagues such as obesity, abuse, terrorism and crime.

When every human being remembers to reconnect mind to Heart, resting in their own natural state, their own inner authority, all desire is naturally fulfilled. Each then radiates the paradise that they are, bringing forth the fruit of authenticity with which to nourish themselves.

On a practical note, our greatest potential for expansion is by mining the treasure trove of what we don't want, the diamond mines of our negative emotion and faulty belief systems. The energy in these is a capped oil well, the pressure of a volcano about to erupt. Recognising and paying attention to such catalytic opportunities will transform your existence. When ignored, the energy rises like a tsunami and destroys you.

Therefore learn to be easy with discomfort, embrace the *atithi,* the uninvited guest. Give the transforming kiss of Beauty to the Beast. See only love, and that is your experience.

Being together in *Satsang,* teaching our mind authentic imagination, inspiring our neglected inner children to dream awake 24/7, these are ways to practical enlightenment, ways to transform our world.

The evolved state is ultimate simplicity... allowing our Heart's desire to unfold, as we return the discriminating mind to its source, to lay down its head in the Heart.

PADA 101
NO PROBLEMS

"If you don't want any problems, don't see any problems, and there won't be any problems!"

This was one of the communications I received from my Inner maybe forty years ago, or more!

It took me half a lifetime to make this Real! To make interruption into a love affair.

Then, of course, I had a lot of unravelling to address. And I could have saved myself so much trouble if I had taken this at face value! Duh!

How do we come to realise there are literally **no mistakes**? That **all** is for love, wellbeing, fulfilment

Of course when we are conditioned to experience disruption, failure, disaster as 'wrong', the instinctual robotic self-contraction happens in the body.

And we lose connection with our early warning system in our instinctual body. A true treasure.

PADA 102
MYSTERY OF LIFE

I am the saviour of my own universe, the Messiah of my myriad selves, the prophet of my own dreaming seeds. I am their strong deliverer from loss and death. I descend into and merge with hell for the sake of my beloved people. Like Jesus, I leave the ninety-nine sheep I already have in the fold, to go after the smallest depressed fragment, my lamb lost in the wasteland.

Structure is created, and merged with, within the womb. Essence becomes form, merges with our genetic inheritance. The Living Word is made flesh and dwells amongst us, in us, as us. As we slowly become aware in the flesh, human consciousness dawns. We experience ourselves and our environment, our world, through the veils of distortion, in a dream or a nightmare, with distant memories of the pristine clarity of the blueprint.

The Ocean of Bliss has yet again taken birth, has merged with form, has become man, woman. God has taken birth to embody Truth, to dream a new dream and enjoy and save another world, to explore and know and love Itself in myriads of myths and dramas.

Another hero risks descent into the abyss as a little child. Essence now experiences itself to actually Be that form, God made man, God made woman. "*And a little child shall lead them*".

I am a multiplicity of Beings and landscapes. I am exploring every aspect of my universe, my own mythology. This particular body was actually born in a maternity ward called Bethlehem.

I am this entire fractaline universe, and I refuse nothing. I am taking possession of My Own Self. I am pure potential unfolding, in form. I am Shiva become Shakti, the avatar of my world, innocence ripening as fruit on the tree.

I am the Mystery of Life tasting and consuming Itself.

13 May 2003

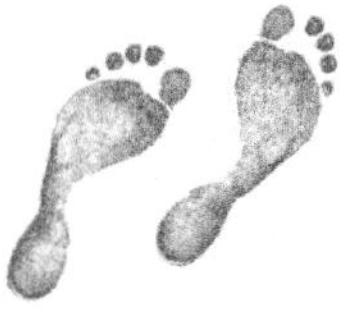

PADA 103
LOVING THE BARDOS

This integration process is interminable. This morning I am witnessing another level that I had forgotten about, almost buried. A descent into hell.

There is a personality here now which is really raw and bleeding. She thinks she is losing it. So much double bind paralyses her. She feels required to do things which are impossible for her, to perform in a way which is alien to her, yet choosing to be part of this environment, she has to perform these tasks.

Madness would be a way out. Collapse makes no difference. Tears make no difference. The environment feels merciless, cold, abrasive. There is no capacity anywhere for gentleness. Hearts are hardened. No one appears to see or hear her, or how it is for her. Beating, punishment or exclusion are the results of inadvertently stepping out of line. Asking for support brings torture. Weakness is death. She feels like her idea of a concentration camp. Injustice is normal here. She keeps very quiet and still. Paralysed by the energy of double bind. Mistakes are punishable by death. Yet she has to seem to act. No action is also punishable by death. She works out a routine of actions which will keep to a middle ground. Fit in with the surroundings. Become a grey ghost, invisible. An automaton in a robotic grey world. Bleeding depressed grey blood. Forced to be a robot.

This is a shadow world. The queues of forgotten, ragged, neglected children. In this body. Ghosts queuing for a crumb of life. What am I seeing? It's as if I am witnessing my childhood. Oh God... was it really like this? It IS still like this, at some level. I have no choice but to see and be in all of this. To witness and consume it gently. But it is interminable. It is hell. My children, my baby selves are in hell. Oh this is a hard place to explore, to love. The bardos are now the half-worlds of neither dead nor alive... Madness would be an escape. *"My cries heave, herds-long..."* It's that Hopkins poem again.

"No worst, there is none. Pitched past pitch of grief"

The energy is a Niagara Falls, a raging fire in my body. I can simply be in it. We can get used to anything. How can I do all these ordinary things... bathing, dressing and greeting Rosie when she comes to clean... yet I do.

I am all of this curious wild story.

Wednesday 13 September 2003

PADA 104
FLOWERS IN THE GARDEN

The Heart of consciousness is merging with matter, taking possession of its physical form, and so old moulds are being shattered and it's just painful!

The physical is becoming conscious of itself as the embodied Heart, and as it does so, it becomes more radiant with bliss. Much of our experience of pain and discomfort is just this, a fuller awareness of the real energetic contraction and distortion, felt ever more deeply in the body. Whatever it may seem to be, it's not getting worse, it's alchemising!

Restricting structure is dissolving. My perception, experience and understanding of what this life is, of what I am looking at, is changing, disintegrating so fast, turning into a complete reversal of how I perceive the world. There seems to be a dissolving of structure, and fresh expression of order, harmony.

What is my Expression? What am I for? I begin to question even more what I am for. What does my continuing expression look like?

Yes! Isn't that the only real question? What is my expression of Being for? I'm deeply curious about the experience of all these other beings. What am I for? Am I simply unfolding? And is there any purpose to it at all? It doesn't matter, but I am really curious about it.

What is 'my' expression and 'your' expression for? For only one thing: to express love, beauty, joy, celebration, humour, lightness, tenderness, for no other reason. And it's not even a reason. Love needs no reason. It is purposeless. Just for joy. Endless enjoyment.

Look, for example, at the infinite entertainment of countless varieties and forms of tropical fish! It's a spontaneous outpouring, like a continuous hug, life embracing itself. The nature of life is to be love, to flow out into form, and the pictures and forms and events we experience are the side effect of that flow, the by-product if you like. Each expression is unique.

As for the difference, well, we are all flowers in the garden and each has its own fragrance, which contributes to the bouquet of the whole. We can't clearly read the seed packets! And so it is a surprise when we learn what we look like, the aroma of our individual fragrance, and our colour. And the appearance is continually evolving, like a little seedling unfurling its leaves. It's not what it looks like though that is of interest, so much as the energy of love with which the flowers dance. And a snowdrop cannot copy, or be, an oak tree. There is no framework of comparison. Every note is different. No two snowflakes are the same. Every expression is unique.

The most vital thing to know is that we are the enjoyers of the perfume and the taste of the fruit. We are not the labourers in the garden. We are the children and the flowers of the gardener. And who is the gardener? Only the Self, the Silent One, the No Thing, which is the mystery of Love itself, the only thing that is Real, and even that One is not doing anything as we experience doing. It is all a spontaneous overflow of the nature of that one.

Do we have any purpose when we open our arms and hug each other when we meet after some time away? It just happens. And does a child at play have any thought or purpose other than just doing what he is doing? Enjoying themselves. That is what Love does - enjoys Itself! Loves Itself. All of Itself.

We are the notes of the little song that the child of Being is humming to itself as it lies at rest, dreaming in the arms of the Divine Mother. This is just a way to describe that total sense of peace and self-absorption of Being in Itself, and the spontaneous outflow of love. There are more intellectual ways to describe it, but unless they have this sense of doodling, this feeling, they miss!

That is why we are always so blissfully happy, like children, when we are thoughtlessly absorbed in doing what we love, in playing with what pleases us, participating in the flow of love into form - dancing, singing, painting, making love, telling stories, walking, enjoying nature.

Allowing ourselves to , in the truest way, the purposeless outflow of love.

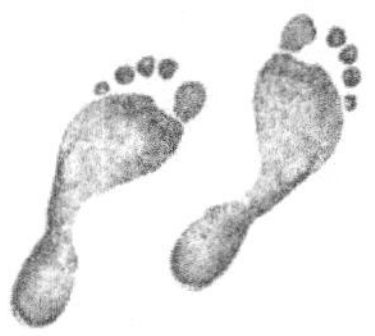

PADA 105
INFINITE DOODLING

I remember, years ago, an experience I had when I was out in the English countryside one hot summer afternoon with Roy. I was standing looking at a very ancient wall, when I was shown many visions. One was of how, at the beginning of time, Love, out of desire to know, feel, touch and taste itself, became a tree, and the leaves were hands and eyes and Hearts with which to know itself, and the leaves were golden in the sun and rain. Each leaf loved the others so much that they gently moved aside to allow the rain to fall on those beneath, and to reflect the sunlight to the others. It's all a beautiful allegory.

The apparent difficulty is that, at a certain level of consciousness or 'enlightenment', the intellect becomes very active, and tries to work out an explanation of a Divine Plan, as if God were a Super Intellect designing it all.

It does seem like that. At the ultimate level, we can only see that the expression of order, beauty and delight into form is a spontaneous display. Love can do no other than express, expand and spontaneously evolve. As the Being of love awakens in form, this process is evolving to an ever more conscious creation. But there really is no personal, individual mind, only a vast open space where it all flows, as in a dream.

You can call it the Silent Witness or Enjoyer of its own infinite doodling or storytelling! And of course the stories are all related with perfect precision to the extent of let-go or surrender.

The spontaneous beauty of freedom of expression into form, without our holding restrictions, is infinitely adorable. However, Being's nature has a childlike simplicity, and loves it ALL without exception.

Years ago when Being was explaining to me on the Inner, I was told "*Shit and Chocolate Pudding are the same in My sight!*" Remember that piece of writing *The Great Way* by the Tenth Zen Patriarch. It starts "*The Great Way is not difficult for those who have no preferences!*"

PADA 106
GODSEEDS

Every human being is a 'godseed', potentially a radiant sun, a whole universe unfolding, just because.

And the unfolding of every seed takes a different course, a unique expression.

It is difficult for the limited perception that is available to see that we cannot compare expressions. We can simply be curious and enjoy ourselves, and choose what we want to become. Stay present. We do not wait to enjoy the unfolding of the never-ending stories.

We are all destined to exit from the collective train, to individualise. Seeds leave the plant so they can grow. And the kaleidoscopic story continues to tell itself in all its variety, fantasy and colour. A vast fairy tale movie.

So, your expression will only be experienced in the moment of its arising, like a child in a state of absorption drawing a picture - unable to say what it is until it is finished. What that expression tastes and looks and feels like, becomes clearer and ever more entertaining as the story goes on unfolding.

You are the witness of your story, at the point of its unfolding. It gets ever finer and ever more entertaining.

So, "*Wait and See!*" as Being is so often saying to us. It's not time for that bit yet!

Don't let's spoil it by trying to second-guess the Divine Soap Opera too much.

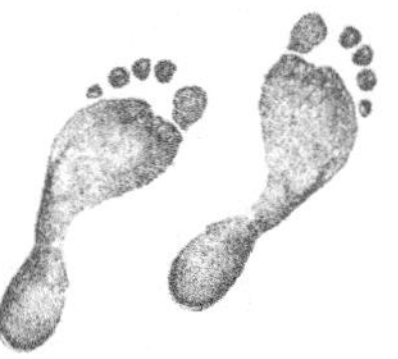

PADA 107
THE ELEGANT DEVI KHULCHIK

So, the story is that this delicate little miniature *Devi* continues to sit here inside this body, her domain, her universe, in her elegant golden sari, bejewelled, very laid back, coolly filing her nails.

I remind her we are going the US at the end of October to co-facilitate the *'Eating raw, living thin'* two-week retreat for women. I suggest that it might seem a little more congruent if we looked a bit more the part. What about adding in a bit of motivation and desire to suit, even a tiny bit more, the model of inspirational fitness that people might be expecting?

She pauses, glances up, and says that great throw-away line, "Am I bovvered?"

I laugh and laugh and laugh! She is so cool. On one level it is completely true. Am I bothered? Yet there is a trace of interest in wearing a form which matches the role. I would prefer to look more the part. I wonder how I am going to play this game!

I sense that if perception were to shift, she might seem to lift a finger and become the compassionate wish-fulfilling goddess that she is in another frame of reference! We, (our royal we), is curious to find a way to get her fully on board, to apparently give a little more attention! What a great game this is. It would be fun to really become an adept and play it the way I see it can be played! With more precision. It's like a pattern of spontaneously drifting clouds. Would be such fun to play instant shapeshifting. I guess more involution is happening.

Integration in this body of the idea of I and me, and her and I and me! The Heart knows there is nothing to say or do. Nothing is really happening, and yet, it is loved, so it is completely Real. Diving deeper into this ocean of bodydream! Right to the centre of my earth. I love this whole story. And that of those who play with me too. I am completely fascinated by this new Baby Devi, this nonchalant, elegant, cool-chick goddess!

So, this must be the way to attend to this diamond-sharp, fairylike creature now appeared in my cast of players. She is very cool and so absolutely together. No mothering about her. She is crisp and contained and laid back, and I might even say self-centred in this form. Total focus on her own stillness, as spontaneous and as clearly herself as a cat.

I want to merge Jeanette with her. I don't know whether she is Kishori or Lalita or Inomina. Not Purnima. Very focused and defined. Streetwise and strong. Young but not naïve at all. Sharp like a well-cut high carat diamond.

After I trained as an enlightenment master with Jake Chapman it must have seemed to me to be better to know how to play here than to do more enlightenment intensives, as I didn't run many of them. I started Heart Communication days instead.

The Power of Reality sits at the computer apparently writing words. This melting and falling away into nothing, this experience of the emptiness beneath the virtual reality skin of things, while this character continues to apparently think and tap away at the keys! This is so obviously the case. What passes for life is *"a thin film on the surface of this vast pulsating living emptiness"*, from my poem.

Some authors are very clear and even funny sometimes. I do love to read them. More bliss to merge with again and again. And it is all already obvious. It's all obvious.

As there is an experience of something in the nothing, I am here to play in it all, just because! As it is all. Endlessly curious about what I seem to be experiencing and being. Constantly updating my playground. From this space I know myself to be a fairy tale, and so that is how it is.

I do love stories. This is one great big popular TV soap opera!

PADA 108
THE WORST?

Sunday evening, 10.20 pm

I drive back here after facilitating an immensely powerful workshop. What to say? Huge energy shifts.

As I drive to Chichester, on the car radio I hear warnings to motorists about rain and thunderstorms along the coast. Before Brighton I hit it. I drive back in a thunderstorm and driving rain. Lightning lighting up the sky, and fear, my worst fear again, and contraction, resistance to circumstances.

But I manage to calm myself and drive with a kind of indifference. I stop producing adrenaline. It was fragile, but I do it! Manage to just be still with the lightning, which used to terrify me. It is continuous with my body.

I ask myself, as I had asked my friend two nights ago, when her daughter-in-law had an emergency C-section and she was having dreams of her grandson being born dead, "What's the worst that can happen?"

1 could be struck by lightning. I could attract it by my fear, and the peculiar energy system 1 have. I

could die. Well, I already gave up my body several times...

It's wonderful how it all settles when I contemplate the worst, with no resistance! Steering into the skid!

I embrace Rahu as the Beloved!

And this is only The Beginning…

SHARING RAHU
Responses to experiencing *The Song of Rahu*

Jo Thilwind, Artist and Writer, Kishori's Murmuration group member

I am blessed to have known Jeanette Kishori for some years now. I originally joined a group she was running online, and have continued to be amazed and inspired by her knowledge. She clearly has a lifetime experience in what I call the 'teachings' of the Mind and the Heart.

I have delved ever more deeply into Jeanette's particular wisdom, experiencing many miracles along the way. One particular event in all my interactions with her stands out above all others. It stopped time as I knew it, took my breath away in awe, wonder and humility, and I knew nothing would ever be the same again. It was my great honour to listen, in sacred space, to Jeanette reciting *The Song of Rahu* to a small group of us. I was transfixed. Her words took on the form of harmonics, multi-layered meanings echoing through the ethers. Their truth going far beyond voice, or language, seeping into my energetic self, my very soul. Shifting me particle by cosmic particle into a new understanding. I understood every word with every cell, although I couldn't have repeated any of it afterwards. It was profound and ethereal all at once.

And in those moments all that I thought dark I could see was light. In all I feared I saw opportunity, kindness and healing. I saw clearly for the first time beauty in that which I so feared within myself. I felt the sorrow of lessons offered and rejected. The sadness of souls' sacrifice to be a ladder for my growth, yet pushed away and ignored. I finally understood that all those painful memories I hid from were shining signposts to where I needed to put my attention, to heal myself so I could be free.

All this was Rahu. But I had turned away from all these gifts, wrapped them in layers of hurt, fear and pain. Then kept them in the dark to know only shame. It was a revelation. I understand this could be challenging to the conscious mind. Difficult to understand, to process. But *The Song of Rahu* sang straight to my soul, and like a gentle breeze, blew the dark clouds away to reveal a clear blue sky. It is a song of soul magick, of truth, of healing, and it resounds in me still.

I am so grateful.

Bright blessings, Jo x

Sue Woodriffe, Body Mind Alchemist, Kishori's Living Alchemy group member

I first heard the recording of *The Song of Rahu* around 2012. I was captivated. I love stories, still with that childlike pleasure when I hear one. The language, flow and rhythm grabbed my attention and delighted me. I could feel an underlying power I did not understand at all.

The Song of Rahu sustained me through a very difficult and dark time in my life. It held me to a truth that was so uncomfortable, but there was no escape, and the more I recognised it, the more I was able to navigate through the murky waters.

At first, I didn't much like the Sanskrit chant, but it has grown on me. The more often I listen, the more I feel an unnamed response deep within me. I have grown to understand the power of sound, and Jeanette has often told me that the words have a transmission in themselves.

Some years later, I was helping Jeanette with her luggage onto a train, when it set off. I had no ticket, no money nor phone on me. The kind guard agreed to let me off at the next station with a note, so I could return to where my car was parked. As I got off the train Jeanette called out "It's the Rahu energy Sue!" I was chuckling to myself. Heaven knows what the other passengers thought!

Patricia Cherry, Life Coach, Kishori's Magickal Heart group member

I'm in love with Rahu. I used to believe that darkness or shadow are to be 'conquered'. However, in the last few years I have realised that there is a better way. Through Jeanette's inspiration I realise that Rahu is the way to process experiences which seem to be a 'disruption'. And I realise that it is the darkness and shadows, those so-called down times, which are the times I grow and learn more about myself, and my evolution into who I really am. So, I am in love with Rahu. My Shadow or darkness, Rahu is certainly decorating my dark times. I now use those times to recognise and honour him.

I was in a state of bewilderment and chronic depression for 70 years, which I believed was due to an upbringing which forced me to be different from my true Self, in order to be acceptable. However, through getting to know Rahu, and accepting the days when I wake feeling depressed, I quickly allow that state and rest with it, move on through my day open-minded, and ask Rahu what I can learn.

I am looking forward so much to having this book on my bedside table. It will be there to decorate the darkness, and celebrate it, like the lights do at the Winter Solstice. It is a never-ending love story.

Rose McClement, Interior Designer, Kishori's Murmuration group member

In the first quarter of 2020 I was drawn to join one of Kishori's community programmes, The Murmuration. Early on, Kishori recited her *Song of Rahu* as an activation. It felt like I was being embraced by an energy that was pulling me into its wake. The words which impact me most powerfully are *"I am the Beloved"*, while, in the same breath, telling of Rahu being the Storm, and all other adversities.

I came to know Rahu as the *Atithi*, the uninvited guest, the Disrupter of all things lurking in the shadows of my life, disturbing, clearing, cleaning, alchemising the dark black coal into gold. Rahu who inspires me to withdraw all projections that I had sent out into the world in different shapes of cruelty, darkness, shame, guilt, fear, pride, apathy. Projections along with their perceptions, beliefs and expectations, behaviour which I had thrown out onto apparent 'others', people, places, circumstances 'out there'.

I realised I was hiding what was lurking in the shadows, dark areas that I did not want to own. Plus, the best is, I had no idea that I had created this darkness, held it in place via Mind! But Rahu did and Rahu does. The Beloved did and The Beloved still does. When The Beloved was coupled with a desire and intention from deep within me to Know My Self and Return to Love, an invitation was sent out to activate Rahu and allow Him to step into my life.

The past three years have been chaotic indeed. Kishori kept saying, "There is no other". Rahu gradually stepped up the pace, and I noticed his signature all over the chaos. Disruption, disturbance, withdrawal of all created pain and suffering as he swept through those dark inner spaces of my being, week after week, month after month. Who would have known that the Rahu activation would take me to these places? Yet I managed to appreciate that Rahu is always The Beloved, with the same intention of Love being the optimal container.

Would I do this again? Hell Yes! This dance with Rahu is far from over. It's ongoing for sure. It doesn't come and go. It is just the intensity of a particular clearing that varies. I would want it no other way. I utterly and completely appreciate all that Rahu the Beloved is.

He is here to stay.

KISHORI'S RAHU REALISATIONS

"The stone that was rejected shall be the cornerstone of the Temple"

This well-known biblical quote emphasises, like Rahu, that the apparently unwanted is, in fact, essential. In no particular order, here are some key realisations from my lifelong experience embodying the essence of *The Song of Rahu*. Not inclusive or exclusive; it is an evolving experience in this game of life, with Rahu as a shepherd prompting the way, or as a lioness tenderly cuffs her cub back onto the safe pathway. Fresh realisations every day, always in the Now, as the carpet of yesterday rolls up behind me.

Actually listening to and feeling the words of *The Song of Rahu* is the best way to experience the clarity. Once these realisations are embodied, life is simplified; a punchline to a joke. The link to the recital is at the back of this book.

1. **All Feeling is precious**.
2. **Acceptance is the start of revision**, the first step to flow.
3. **Revise it all** to match your expression of love.
4. **Radiate only this freedom of love**.

5. **Allow the Yogic Flowers to fill your garden,** and enjoy the fruit.
6. **Focus on your Blueprint**.
7. **Contemplate your HeartStar**.
8. **There is no Other**. All is One consciousness, a holographic living omnipresent Intelligence whose nature is Love, whose centre is everywhere and circumference nowhere.
9. **The One plays all the parts in the game**. This Intelligence is what I actually am. It is the true identity of each one.
10. **I am the Source and cause of my life**. Without exception, everywhere, always, already.
11. **Love your whole story**. Every tiniest detail.
12. **Rahu is the shepherd**, guiding ourselves back to ourselves, since there is only the One.
13. **Our destiny is to distinguish the Real from the unreal**.
14. **Rahu calls us to radical withdrawal of projection**, since there is no Other.
15. **All this is expression**. Love knows no comparison, no judgement, no assumptions, no mistakes, no good, no bad, no right, no wrong, no loss or lack.
16. **A house divided cannot stand**. The smallest distinction or prejudice creates separation, and sets Heaven and Earth forever apart.
17. **Life in truth is either easy, or impossible**.

18. **There is only love; only what we love is Real**. Love is biased in our favour as we can imagine our fairy godmother might feel, besotted, *"pressed down and overflowing"*.

19. **In the One consciousness there are infinite dimensions**, beyond limits, such as death and birth. Those thresholds are illusory. We are not born, and can never die.

20. **We experience what we put attention on**, so select focus carefully.

21. **There is no fiction**. Anything that can be imagined can come into form.

22. **'Luck' and 'fate' are unreal**, we are designed to choose. Nothing 'happens' to us. There are no 'circumstances beyond our control'.

23. **Rahu invites us to allow** our loving imagination to dream new, full-spectrum, beyond the time-space bubble.

24. **Time is not linear or fixed**, as explored in quantum physics. We can revise the 'past' and imagine the 'future'. It's all Now.

25. **Each one is Source, bringing Heaven to Earth**. Revision with intention, feeling and imagination changes anything. *"Behold I make all things new"*.

26. **Steady practice expands and refines the art of choosing**, establishing innate knowing.

27. **The experience is unique for each of us** as individual living Intelligence.

28. **Obstacles are necessary to make our realisation perfect**. Whenever conscious direction is interrupted, this is a Rahu intervention. It heralds the way forward, a wave breaking, a portal to open.

29. **In a Rahu moment be curious**, recognise and acknowledge feeling and welcome the interruption. Relax into the HeartField and allow revision. Choose to see it differently. The darkest moment is just before the dawn.

30. **Allow** inner vision, choice and spontaneous expression from the HeartField. 'Strategy' or externally-motivated 'doing to get' cannot succeed.

31. **Rahu interrupts linear ways of thinking;** avoid following apparent 'logic', Rahu invites revision, transformation and completion.

32. **All energy has to return to source**, so every desire is satisfied, like bungee- jumping.

33. **Rahu inspires our new way of Being**, a game of hide-and-seek with Self, a never-ending living theatre. All the players, Red Riding Hood and the Wolf, stand hand-in-hand to take a bow together at the end of the pantomime, as One.

34. **Revise, or you'll get the old default**.

35. **Be the Union of Opposites**, the ultimate source of power.

36. **Go to the place of the no-thing**, design and update expression of your Blueprint. Use your conscious mind to design what you really want.
37. **Be constantly curious**, honouring Rahu as the Beloved, allowing your awareness to expand beyond anything you can currently imagine. It's a never-ending story.
38. **This is only The Beginning** of this never-ending love story, aligning experience with intention.

You're welcome to note any further Rahu Realisations you may have here:

ABOUT KISHORI JEANETTE MCKENZIE

Life is a fairy tale. The stories I tell have no deep significance. They are gossamer tales, as light as wisps of clouds drifting in the breeze on a summer's day. They are like life, totally unimportant, and yet full of juice for those whose heart knows how to drink. Fairy tales were never intended to improve your mind or help you in any way at all. The best you can do for a human child or a little nut tree is never to help, or try to improve, but simply to enjoy the pleasure of their company. For of what use is a silver nutmeg or a child but for the sake of the joy they bring? My stories are therefore simply for my own entertainment.

I have always lived in two worlds: the busy prosaic life lived by adults, which they mostly didn't appear to enjoy, to which it seemed I was expected to conform, and in which I was often miserable; and then there was my secret inner life, the truly magical golden life of my childhood, the thread of which somehow still remains unbroken to this day. Amazingly so, for it seems that the process of growing up places us relentlessly and inevitably under a spell, behind prison bars of defining mind, erasing the secret child life of innocence, and the experience of being immersed in nature, and being at one with all things. These first two paragraphs are from my forthcoming memoir, *The Silver Nutmeg*.

What can I say about the I am that I am, the Nameless One, Source and fullness of my life as Jeanette, Kishori and many other names? I am engaged in the play of consciously loving this whole story. The love affair between the Unknown and the Known, the indescribable yoga of the *Hieros Gamos* in every precious *"drop of liquid life"*.

The non-linear realisation of this holographic life is reflected in my poetry. Everything and anything, and anything in between. There is no separation between 'ordinary' and 'extraordinary'. 'I Am' loves it all, as a child loves its scribbled drawing. Not just the extraordinary events, which do not happen in 3D life, the Magickal life is either easy or impossible. I find it so. A pattern of drifting clouds, where the edges are blurred. The unplanned, that which intervenes, the Keyala moments, spontaneous, beyond conscious control.

My 'inner life' is my alchemical journey. It is what I really came here to do, to play and discover what Jung calls "The Treasure Hard to Attain", which all the yogic flowers and fruit grow from.

Divorce, death, alienation, misunderstanding, I explored the experience of loss and rejection. As a child brought up Catholic I asked to follow the way of the cross of Jesus, but eventually I was ordered to leave the church by Jesus! And my Being forbids me to join any other 'system'!

Each one of us has our own unique imprint and conditioning to unravel, to love it all into the wholeness that it already IS. There is no separation, no good, no bad. As *The Great Way* says, *"Make the smallest distinction, however, and heaven and earth are set infinitely apart"*.

I experienced many epiphanies where my Magickal mystical life and my apparently prosaic conflicted life became one, and the hard edges of the 'separative life' dissolved. Driving my car straight through a solid oncoming car. On the bus in Leicester aged 14, when I experienced the bus seat and everything becoming the body of God. When I found the *Avadhuta Gita* in the Ramakrishna Math in Bangalore, India, and spent the day reading and weeping in realisation, *"Forgive me Lord for worshipping you in the temple"*.

Life appeared to swing between these two states. The way I knew it to be, the way I experienced, and the way it is, in a kind of metastable equilibrium. I saw the world as candyfloss, light beams, flow. I had the thought that all I had to do was to tell the world, and know it into wholeness, through baby eyes, and so it would be!

Puzzled by the experienced discrepancy between my inner and outer worlds, I sold my residential retreat centre, and went travelling. In India I found a few places where the veil was so thin, transparent, blissful. Heaven on earth. I would spend all day lying in bliss in the little Shiva cave, head to the ground.

I am space, with points of light emerging. Constantly refining my changes. Allowing. I am curious about who I, the I that is We, is becoming. I had an experience of giving birth to the earth, as if it were my baby. Being a Mother is the ultimate experience in Duality. I am Shiva and Shakti merging, in the never-ending story of awakening to myself. Epiphanies every day. Superfluid. A pattern of drifting clouds, defining and refining, it's all holographic. Constantly forming and reforming. The carpet of experience is always rolling up behind me as I walk.

Kishori Jeanette McKenzie's adventure in consciousness is ongoing. Ever curious and relentlessly inquiring, she is an engaging alchemist, entertainer, story-teller, poet, Humanistic Psychologist, Yoga and Polarity Practitioner, playing the game of Life in the HeartField.

Founder of Magick Makeover, Quantum Reality Training and the McKenzie Boalch Foundation, since early childhood she has been constantly investigating how the world works, the nature of consciousness and expression of feeling, combining eastern wisdom with western communication skills, alchemy and yoga to create a unique invitation to Self-Inquiry.

Realising that unseen, unused energy and talent distorts and disturbs, Kishori enjoys facilitating the discovery and integration of these untapped resources, naturally enabling a renewed energy flow and dramatically increased performance and satisfaction in individuals, leaders, their organisations and their lives. It's one of her greatest joys when they see the punchline.

Kishori says: "The simple clarity of Being emerges from a continual integration of the depth of love in the Quantum HeartField. This innate presence is catalytic and irresistible. Whatever I think I might know is as nothing in the face of this vast simplicity. This practice of Self-Inquiry is designed to be effortless. I absolutely love allowing that simple presence to fill the space, and then watching miraculous transformations unfold."

A natural linguist with love of communication and travel, at an early age Jeanette became fluent in and taught several European languages. Always drawn to particularly support those who struggle most, she calls us to embrace Rahu as the Beloved, and thrive. Resonating with the frequency of Jesus's words *"I am come to make the blind to see, the deaf to hear, to heal the broken-hearted"*, she applied her brilliant originality and creativity with very successful results running, amongst other projects, a Youth Training Scheme, always finding in-the-moment ways to touch their hearts and inspire. Practical activation and application of her profound experiences touch everything she turns to.

Precise use of language is vital in spearheading the culture shift heralded by *The Song of Rahu.* Coming soon is Kishori's book exploring how the words we use to express ourselves reinforce our beliefs, define or limit our experience. When we have true clarity and balance, it's all easy. Impossible doesn't come into it.

A pioneer in the field, she established her own retreat centre for development of human potential, creating processes for authentic communication, and transforming perception, *Designer Software for the Evolutionary Mind.* Giving voice to words expressing true desire, bypassing the cognitive mind, declaring and activating the Heart's desire, our innate power, with pristine focus. Creating a Magickal world, with a particular skill for presenting the potentially challenging in a relatable, down-to-earth way, always with a smile. Facilitating life-changing events, and delivering cutting edge keynote talks.

Kishori has a daughter and a son, who have both developed into leaders in their fields, living many of her dreams in England and India; and four grandchildren, two in India, two in the UK. Her particular interests include nutrition and embodiment, which she has explored extensively, and finding balance between the key aspects of Life. She also delights in aesthetic design, and precise colour combination.

Distilling all her experience, she is developing her unique inner-inspired spontaneous Keyala Yoga. She is intending to offer it in groups and on individually tailored programmes, online and near her home in Tavistock, Devon, on the edge of Dartmoor, in south west England.

New programmes and events are constantly being developed. Updates and more details about where to start your Living Alchemy adventure with Kishori Jeanette McKenzie can be found on https://www.magick-makeover.com/start/.

ALSO BY KISHORI JEANETTE MCKENZIE

Forthcoming Mahadevi Press publications

Designer Software for the Evolutionary Mind
The Call: An introduction to Living Alchemy

Are You Ready for a Magick Makeover?
Resources for Self-Inquiry

Glimpses of Treasure Eyeland
Poetry of embodiment

Your Magickal Notebook
To anchor Living on Purpose in Living Alchemy

The Silver Nutmeg
The extraordinary memoir of an adventurer in consciousness

Miranda and the Firedragon
A timeless fairy tale

The Coming of the Dark Ones
Celebrating Rahu, a contemporary fairy tale

GLOSSARY FOR RAHU

A selection of terms as I use them, many taken from Sanskrit, in alphabetical order.

Alchemy is a process of transformation, shifting from the current cosmic display to one in alignment with the Heart's choice

Amrit, Sanskrit for the nectar of immortality

Asuras, Sanskrit for demons

Atithi, Sanskrit for outside time. An unexpected visitor. The beggar at the feast. A place is laid for the uninvited guest at meals in India. Guest is god. And the beggar at any moment is likely to transform into Krishna, the supreme god

Buddh is Buddha, a god

Buddhi is the light at the doorway, the intellect

Candyfloss is what I see on experiencing the nature of everything as filaments of light, pure consciousness

Cat's cradle refers to the apparent complications, muddles in our lives, to be unravelled in own unique way

Desire is from the Latin root *de sidere* – from the stars

Devas or **Devis**, Sanskrit for gods

Dyad, Heart Communication with a partner

Gunas, Sanskrit for qualities, referring to nature's three energetic forces which weave together to form the universe and everything in it. The three are *sattva* (goodness, calmness, harmony), *rajas* (passion, activity, movement) and *tamas* (inertia, laziness, ignorance)

Heart Communication is communication in the HeartField, rooted in feeling, beyond the cognitive mind, with unconditional listening. A profound expression of our true desire

HeartField is the energy field of the 'Heart'. The Heart is the master alchemist, it feeds on 'darkness', continually consuming and replacing. Incoherence does not exist in the HeartField. Always aligned with precision to the 'coherent blueprint', allowing the Shift

Heart Inquiry is inquiry in the HeartField, beyond the cognitive mind

Hermes Trismegistus is the thrice-great Master of Alchemy

Hieros Gamos is the sacred marriage or union, with self, or the union of the conscious and unconscious

Homa, a sacred fire ceremony in Vedic tradition

Kalpataru is the wish-fulfilling tree in Sanskrit

Kapalbhati is a cleansing and energising breathing technique in yoga

Keyala is a spontaneous whim or fancy. Impulse. A Bengali word that I first learnt through Sri Anandamayi Ma, a revered Bengali saint. Her way of being was surrendered to the impulse of the Heart. She would wake and, following her impulse, would simply walk to the station and get on a train. To Bangalore for example! Like a child. And circumstances would configure to support her every action! I am not suggesting you spread your wings and fly from the roof tops, but with a certain state of realisation this holographic dream of ours responds

Kishori is a cutting-edge frequency, singer and dancer who never grows old. The name was given me by Osho

Krishna is a supreme Hindu deity, god of protection, compassion, tenderness, and love. My son has become known as Krishna in India

Kundalini, a Rahu energy, the rising feminine force

Magick is the alchemical perception shift which gives an ever-new perspective

Mahadevi is the Great Goddess in Sanskrit

Mala is the traditional number of 108 prayer beads

Naga Vasuki the snake who stiffened his body to stir the amrit in the Sanskrit myth

Padas are footsteps in Sanskrit, glimpses or moments in time

Puja a worship ritual to the deities

Rahu is one of the nine planetary deities in Vedic astrology. He's a shadow graha, not a body, but an absence of a body, a moveable feast. He has a hidden influence, from the unknown, unseen. He is closely connected with the phases of the moon. The myth is told on the recording of my recital

Sadhana is practice, usually spiritual

Samskaras, residual negative impressions which leave a scar

Samyama is binding together, concentration

Sandhya is Sanskrit for twilight

Shadow is a common way of describing the unseen, unknown, unconscious aspects

Shiva is a Supreme Being, and one of the principal deities of Hinduism

Uroboric is cyclical, self-devouring, from an ancient symbol depicting a serpent or dragon eating its own tail. I use it to mean a natural state of complete absorption in self

Yab-yum is a symbol depicting union of a male and a female deity, representing the primordial union of wisdom and compassion

Yoga is union, in perfect equilibrium

Yogic Flowers are the innate fulfilment of life, the stated aims, loosely translated as Dharma, purpose, Artha, wealth, Kama, pleasure and Moksha, freedom (see my www.magick-makeover.com website for more details)

Published by Mahadevi Press
Tavistock, Devon, UK

FREE BONUSES

LISTEN TO KISHORI'S RECITAL OF THE SONG OF RAHU

The Song of Rahu is an extraordinary incantation, a powerful affirmation that all is simply the Beloved. In the midst of the darkest circumstances, the rhythm of this Song resonates as a sruti note. Its uniquely haunting beauty, together with the profound realisation of the author as she speaks, take the mind beyond fear to rest in the Truth of the non-dual state.

I invite you to listen, hand on Heart, and to viscerally experience and feel the words, bypassing the cognitive mind.

This powerful activation is password protected.

Enter the password **Mahadevi** for access.

https://www.kishori.net/rahu-recital

FREE EBOOK DOWNLOAD

A Gift from Kishori Jeanette McKenzie

Designer Software for the Evolutionary Mind

The Call: Introduction to Living Alchemy

https://www.magick-makeover.com/designer-software

Blank pages for personal notes.

Q&A sessions will be held. Details in The Song of Rahu Book private Facebook group, which you're invited to join as a reader of this book.

You're welcome to also share your insights and observations there about dancing with *The Song of Rahu*

https://www.facebook.com/groups/thesongofrahubook

Printed in Great Britain
by Amazon

19755329R00193